The Gospel Of St. John

You are holding a reproduction of an original work that is in the public domain in the United States of America, and possibly other countries. You may freely copy and distribute this work as no entity (individual or corporate) has a copyright on the body of the work. This book may contain prior copyright references, and library stamps (as most of these works were scanned from library copies). These have been scanned and retained as part of the historical artifact.

This book may have occasional imperfections such as missing or blurred pages, poor pictures, errant marks, etc. that were either part of the original artifact, or were introduced by the scanning process. We believe this work is culturally important, and despite the imperfections, have elected to bring it back into print as part of our continuing commitment to the preservation of printed works worldwide. We appreciate your understanding of the imperfections in the preservation process, and hope you enjoy this valuable book.

THE GOSPEL OF ST. JOHN

Works by the same Author.

THE PSALMS, Vol. I. Crown 8vo, cloth, 7s. 6d.

THE EPISTLE TO THE COLOSSIANS. Cloth 8vo, 7s. 6d.

BIBLE CLASS EXPOSITIONS.

THE GOSPEL OF ST. MATTHEW, Vols. I. and II. Crown 8vo, cloth, 3s. 6d. each.

THE GOSPEL OF ST. LUKE, Vol. III. Crown 8vo, cloth, 3s. 6d.

LONDON:
HODDER & STOUGHTON, 27, PATERNOSTER ROW.

THE
GOSPEL OF ST. JOHN

BY

ALEXANDER MACLAREN, D.D.

𝔏𝔬𝔫𝔡𝔬𝔫
HODDER AND STOUGHTON
27 PATERNOSTER ROW

MDCCCXCIII

Printed by *Hazell, Watson, & Viney, Ld.*, London and Aylesbury.

PREFACE

THESE chapters were written as a commentary on the International Sunday School Lessons for the American *Sunday School Times*, from which they are reprinted with the concurrence of the proprietors.

CONTENTS

LESS.		PAGE
I.	THE WORD IN ETERNITY, TIME, AND FLESH	1
	St. John i. 1-18.	
II.	TWO DAYS: JOHN'S LAST, AND CHRIST'S FIRST	11
	St. John i. 29-42.	
III.	THE FIRST RAY OF THE GLORY	20
	St. John ii. 1-11.	
IV.	"HOW CAN THESE THINGS BE?"	29
	St. John iii. 1-17.	
V.	THE THIRSTY GIVER OF LIVING WATER	39
	St. John iv. 5-26.	
VI.	THE LIFE-GIVER AND JUDGE	49
	St. John v. 17-30.	
VII.	BREAD ENOUGH, AND TO SPARE	58
	St. John vi. 1-14.	
VIII.	TRUE WORK FOR TRUE BREAD	66
	St. John vi. 26-40.	
IX.	"THAT ROCK WAS CHRIST"	76
	St. John vii. 31-44.	
X.	FREEDOM AND SONSHIP	85
	St. John viii. 31-47.	
XI.	JESUS SEEING THE BLIND, AND THE BLIND SEEING JESUS	95
	St. John ix. 1-11, 35-38.	
XII.	THE SHEPHERD OF MEN	103
	St. John x. 1-16.	

Contents

LESS.		PAGE
XIII.	THE CROWNING MIRACLE	112
	St. John xi. 21-44.	
XIV.	WHAT JESUS THOUGHT ABOUT THE CROSS	121
	St. John xii. 20-36.	
XV.	THE MASTER-SERVANT	130
	St. John xiii. 1-17.	
XVI.	THE PRESENT-ABSENT CHRIST AND THE ABIDING COMFORTER	139
	St. John xiv. 1-3, 15-27.	
XVII.	THE VINE AND THE BRANCHES	149
	St. John xv. 1-16.	
XVIII.	THE SPIRIT CONVINCING THE WORLD AND GUIDING THE CHURCH.	158
	St. John xvi. 1-15.	
XIX.	THE INTERCESSOR	169
	St. John xvii. 1-19.	
XX.	THE WILLING PRISONER	180
	St. John xviii. 1-13.	
XXI.	THE RELUCTANT JUDGE, THE RESOLVED ACCUSERS, AND THE PATIENT CHRIST	189
	St. John xix. 1-16.	
XXII.	"IT IS FINISHED"	198
	St. John xix. 17-30.	
XXIII.	THE DAWNINGS OF FAITH IN THE RISEN LORD	207
	St. John xx. 1-18.	
XXIV.	THE SEA AND THE SHORE	216
	St. John xxi. 1-14.	
XXV.	REVIEW LESSON THOUGHTS	223

LESSON I

The Word in Eternity, Time, and Flesh

St. John i. 1-18

1. "In the beginning was the Word, and the Word was with God, and the Word was God.
2. The same was in the beginning with God.
3. All things were made by Him; and without Him was not any thing made that was made.
4. In Him was life; and the life was the light of men.
5. And the light shineth in darkness; and the darkness comprehended it not.
6. There was a man sent from God, whose name was John.
7. The same came for a witness, to bear witness of the Light, that all men through Him might believe.
8. He was not that Light, but was sent to bear witness of that Light.
9. That was the true Light, which lighteth every man that cometh into the world.
10. He was in the world, and the world was made by Him, and the world knew Him not.
11. He came unto His own, and His own received Him not.
12. But as many as received Him, to them gave He power to become the sons of God, even to them that believe on His name:
13. Which were born, not of blood, nor of the will of the flesh, nor of the will of man, but of God.
14. And the Word was made flesh, and dwelt among us, (and we beheld His glory, the glory as of the only begotten of the Father,) full of grace and truth.
15. John bare witness of Him, and cried, saying, This was He of whom I spake, He that cometh after me is preferred before me: for He was before me.
16. And of His fulness have all we received, and grace for grace.
17. For the law was given by Moses, but grace and truth came by Jesus Christ.
18. No man hath seen God at any time; the only begotten Son, which is in the bosom of the Father, He hath declared Him."

THE simplest words carry the deepest meanings. These brief sentences of this wonderful prologue are as inexhaustible in thought as they are inartificial in language. They unveil the eternal depths of Deity, and gather all the history of man in time into one long process of the effluent light warring with darkness, which culminates in the incarnate Word, "the Light," whose name at last is disclosed as Jesus Christ, the fountain of all grace and truth, the only declarer of God. Volumes could not worthily set forth the truths condensed in these verses. Eighteen centuries have but spelled out a little of the meaning of these eighteen verses. Heaven will not exhaust them.

It is a mistake to try to force the style of John into logical grooves. The great stones with which he builds are laid on each other without mortar. The links of connection are so numerous that each new student finds some fresh one. And they are all there, and more besides; for the mighty facts which he tells in such childlike, deep speech are all laced together by innumerable ties. We may, however, note that the two references to the Baptist's testimony, which break in upon the flow of the evangelist's thought, seem to part it into distinct portions, and to be themselves distinct. If we read straight on, omitting John's two sayings, the stream is continuous. We follow, then, this clue to a division of the subject-matter, not, however, laying stress on it.

I. Verses 1-5, then, begin by carrying us out of time and creation, to unveil to our awestruck vision something of the eternal depths of God, when none but God was, and thence descend to reveal how things came to be, how a universe has life, how what is but life in other creatures rises in man to be light, and how, through all the ages, the uncreated light has striven with the intrusive and obstinate darkness. God in Himself, creation, preservation, and the whole history of man as moral, intellectual, and spiritual, are here. "In the beginning God *created*," but "in the beginning the Word *was*." When creatures began to be, He was there already. That necessarily implies eternal existence. John does not speak as if his terms needed definition. Either they were already familiar to his readers, or he felt that his statements sufficiently explained them. This at least is clear, that the three clauses of the first verse set forth the Word as eternal, as a Person holding communion with God, and as Himself Divine in nature.

At the close of the prologue he will identify this eternal, Divine, personal Word with his dear Lord and Master, but now he simply affirms, in that strangely assured and yet quiet way of his, as if no proof were needed. If we accept these words, we shall be wiser than all philosophers, and have got nearer the heart of things than they. The second verse forms the transition to the activity of the Word in history. It gathers the three clauses preceding into one, and thus presents that Word as fitted for the work to be next ascribed to Him.

That work is, first, creation. Mark the contrast of the ante-temporal "was" of the first verse and the "came to be" ("were made") of the third verse. Observe, too, the universality of the Word's creative energy, as twice signalised in the two clauses. Note the specific form of His action. "Through Him" (not "by") teaches, as in Colossians i. 16 and other passages, that the Word is the agent of creation, while the Father is the source. Observe also the distinction between "through" and "not apart from," or "without." The one presents Him as the agent; the other insists on His presence with His creation as necessary to its existence, and forbids us to think of it as being like a man's work, capable of subsisting away from its maker. It is the same teaching as Paul's in Colossians i. 17: "In Him all things consist." Observe, too, the difference of tense, "*was* made" and "*hath been* made," the former expressing the original creative act, the latter the continuous existence of the things created.

If we keep to the division of verses in both the Authorised and the Revised Versions, verse four rises in the scale of being, and shows how not only inanimate things came to be, but living things to live. The change of preposition is significant. "Through Him" and "not apart from Him" express a less close and wonderful relation than "in Him." Life is a gift implying a closer resemblance to its source than inanimate matter attains. "With Thee is the fountain of life." Science is baffled to tell what life is, and still more to produce it. John's words go nearer the centre than any biology has reached.

"In Him was life"—not, of course, meaning that He lives, but that He gives life. Then we rise still higher, to the one creature who has self-conscious life, and can turn himself partly round to catch a glimpse of the source. "Light" is one of John's great, simple words, which open out into unfathomable depths. Physical light divides into three chief sets of beams. "The light of men" does the same; for we need not ask whether it means purity, knowledge, or joy, since it means all, and these three are really one. All that makes us men, rising above the less conscious forms of life, which are too low for morality or knowledge, and may be happy but not blessed, and above inanimate being, flows from the same hand which created and sustains.

May there not be in that singular "was" of the fourth verse some faint gleam of the vanished Eden, where God's idea of manhood was for a moment realised, and, in unbroken communion, life was light? The abrupt introduction, in the next verse, of "darkness," hints at some catastrophe unnamed, to account for its appearance. And so the sad history of humanity is summed up in verse five as a continual meek shining of the light, side by side with its opposite, and, if we adopt the rendering in the text of the Revised Version, a continual resistance by the darkness; or, if we take the margin, a continual shining of the light in spite of resistance. There is a paradox. Light dispels darkness. The two cannot co-exist, but this light and darkness can and do. In these few broad outlines the whole history of man is condensed, up to John Baptist.

II. John's mission is regarded in verses 6-8 in its relation to that light which is not yet presented as historically manifested in Jesus. He, like all the prophets whose missions may be summed up in his, was but "a man," who, like "all things," began to be. (Note that the "was" of verse six is the same as "were made" of verse three, and not the same as "was" of verse one.) His office was to witness of it, being himself not light, but lighted; the scope of his mission was universal, and its purpose the production of "belief." A pregnant contrast is implied throughout. The description of John fits Jesus, unless Jesus is what this Gospel proclaims Him, the incarnate Light. Otherwise He too was but sent to point away from Himself.

III. The section between the two utterances of the Baptist deals with the incarnation under the two aspects of the coming of the Light and the becoming flesh of the Word, thus knitting together the two thoughts of the first section. The former representation includes verses nine to thirteen; the latter, verse fourteen. In the former part, verses nine and ten still retain some reference to the action of the light before the incarnation. Verse nine is ambiguous, but "coming into the world" is a standing expression for the incarnation, and is therefore most naturally referred to "the true light." The existence of the "true light," as distinguished from imperfect realisations or reflections of it, such as John, the universal action of the light on humanity, and the culmination thereof in a historical "coming," are the great truths in the ninth verse. But, before elaborating the last further, the writer pauses for a moment on the same sad thought as in verse five. "I speak of a 'coming,' but it is of One who was here before He 'came,' had been here ever since He made this world, and had been moving unrecognised among men, like a king incognito." That was not because He hid Himself, but because the darkness would have none of the light. The need for a further coming is laid in the failure of the former, "being in the world," to bring recognition.

All the preceding has been a majestic flight of stairs from heaven to earth, and now we reach the foot. The Light who was, "came," as John too "came," in so far as both had a historical beginning and appeared among men; but the Light came, as this whole Gospel teaches, in an altogether unique sense, as by His own will, and from a previous state of being. "His own land" was stripping His forerunner, because He was before he came.

Finally, verses 16-18 gather up the blessed issues of incarnation, contrast these with previous revelation, and, at last, declare how all the glorious names of Word, Light, and Son meet in the man Jesus Christ. The close connection of the first words with those of verse fourteen shows that the stream of thought goes on, overleaping the reference to the Baptist. Christ's "fulness" is the perfect completeness of Divine powers with which He is, so to speak, charged, and that fulness is a communicative fulness. The personal experience of the Apostle and his brethren comes in to attest that. Those who can say, "We have received of it," need no arguments beside to prove Him Divine. Those who "receive Him" (ver. 12) do therein "receive" all spiritual gifts. The grace of this moment, if used aright, is ever exchanged for new grace, and that in increasing richness.

The law was given, in one definite act, as an external and authoritative statute, fixed and rigid; but what Jesus brings "comes to be through Him," for ever flowing out in a vital process and taking shape in men's hearts. The contents of the law are statutes, those of Christ's gift are love bestowed and bestowing, and truth, even the light from the Light, and speech from the Word.

So Jesus Christ is disclosed as both Word and Light, is set far above all messengers of God, is the Divine communicator to men of all the Divine fulness, and the source of all grace and truth. In one last sentence this fisherman-apostle transcends all philosophy, and lays the foundation stone of all true theology and of all the satisfaction of the needs of humble souls. The limitations of our powers make the direct knowledge of God impossible for man. The manhood of Him who in and from eternity was the Word, and from the beginning has been the light of men, makes it certain that the invisible God is fully declared in Him, who in timeless union is "in the bosom of the Father," and who yet tabernacled among us, that the eyes which could not see God might calmly and lovingly "behold His glory," and in gazing might not only behold, but possess, the grace and truth of which He is full, and of which the world without Him is empty.

LESSON II

Two Days: John's Last and Christ's First

St. John i. 29-42

29. "The next day John seeth Jesus coming unto him, and saith, Behold the Lamb of God, which taketh away the sin of the world.

30. This is He of whom I said, After me cometh a man which is preferred before me: for He was before me.

31. And I knew Him not: but that He should be made manifest to Israel, therefore am I come baptizing with water.

32. And John bare record, saying, I saw the Spirit descending from heaven like a dove, and it abode upon Him.

33. And I knew Him not: but He that sent me to baptize with water, the same said unto me, Upon whom thou shalt see the Spirit descending, and remaining on Him, the same is He which baptizeth with the Holy Ghost.

34. And I saw, and bare record that this is the Son of God.

35. Again the next day after John stood, and two of his disciples;

36. And looking upon Jesus as He walked, he saith, Behold the Lamb of God!

37. And the two disciples heard him speak, and they followed Jesus.

38. Then Jesus turned, and saw them following, and saith unto them, What seek ye? They said unto Him, Rabbi, (which is to say, being interpreted, Master,) where dwellest Thou?

39. He saith unto them, Come and see. They came and saw where He dwelt, and abode with Him that day: for it was about the tenth hour.

40. One of the two which heard John speak, and followed Him, was Andrew, Simon Peter's brother.

41. He first findeth his own brother, Simon, and saith unto him, We have found the Messias, which is, being interpreted, the Christ.

42. And he brought him to Jesus. And when Jesus beheld him, He said, Thou art Simon the son of Jona: thou shalt be called Cephas, which is by interpretation, A stone."

THE careful notes of time in this and the next chapter show that Jesus had returned from the temptation to the place where John was baptizing before the testimony of the latter here recorded. John i. 26 seems to show that Jesus was in the crowd when the deputation from Jerusalem came; but, at all events, the first part of the lesson deals with John's new witness to Him (vers. 29-34), while the second part gives the effect of that testimony in the transference of the first disciples from John to Jesus. These two days witnessed the beginning of the greatest institution in the world,—the Christian Church,—and the end of prophecy, which reached its goal when its last representative stood in the presence of Jesus, and, with pointing finger, designated Him as the Lamb of God. To outward seeming they were but a little knot of poor Jews. How kings and Cæsars would have scoffed, if told that they were the nucleus of a movement which would shatter their thrones and reshape the world! "The kingdom of God cometh not with observation."

The testimony of the Baptist, as recorded in this section, is singularly unlike his preaching as reported in the Synoptic Gospels. Here it points specifically to the person of Jesus as the Messiah, and speaks a new insight into His character and work. He is not here the Judge with fan in hand, but the Lamb taking away sin. This difference has been used as an argument against the truth of this Gospel; but there is nothing suspicious or doubtful about it, if we only remember that the other Gospels give John's preaching as it rang in men's ears before the baptism of Jesus, while this Gospel gives it as it was after that baptism had opened his eyes to the person of the Messiah, and the descent of the dove had taught him the inmost nature of Messiah's rule and power.

The Baptist himself tells the process of his new vision, in this section, and certainly the cause assigned by him is adequate to the effect. No wonder that, when he beheld "the Spirit descending like a dove and abiding" on the unknown man's head, his heart leaped up to recognise his Lord, and his stern spirit was bowed in lowly adoration. The interval during which Jesus was tempted in the wilderness gave John's new knowledge time to clear itself. Hence the eager swiftness of his testimony when he saw Jesus coming to him, as if calling on him for homage and witness. It is not addressed to any particular hearer, but is a public proclamation.

The point of the comparison with "the Lamb" is not in character, but in office. The explanation which takes it to mean innocence, patience, meekness, is miserably shallow, and is negatived by the following clause, which puts all the stress of comparison on taking away the world's sin. Where did John get this comparison? There are three distinct sources in the Old Testament, all tributary to this saying. There is the lamb of history, when Abraham steadied his voice to answer, "My son, God will provide Himself a lamb." The Lamb of God is God-provided. There is the lamb of ritual, both that offered daily and that of the passover, which feast was near when John spoke. There is the lamb of prophecy, set forth in Isaiah's great prophecy, which is clearly in John's mind. There the ideas of unresisting meekness and of vicarious sacrifice are clearly expressed, and in the light of these we cannot but see that the "taking away the sin of the world" by the sacrifice of Himself is the very purpose for which God has provided the Lamb. Note the universality of the power of that sacrifice,—"the world." Note the completeness of its efficacy as dealing with "sin," the whole mass as a whole, and not only with "sins" separately. Note the hint of the manner of its operation in "taketh away," which implies removal by Himself bearing the burden. Note that not only the punishment, but the reality of sin, is removed. How clear the insight of John, then. And yet this is he who could send to ask, "Art Thou He that should come?" Let us beware lest mists born of our own hearts wrap the brightest stars of truth in a doleful film!

Verses thirty and thirty-one glow with thankful triumph and lowly recognition of inferiority. Few prophets have the joy of saying, "This is He of whom I spoke." At such an hour of fulfilment the true prophet recalls with thankfulness his words, spoken when no sign of their accomplishment was visible, and he knew as little as any by whom they were to be brought to pass. Well for those who can thus recall unashamed their faith and testimony when they stand before Christ. Very beautifully does John recall his witness borne when the person of the Messiah was unknown to him, his confidence even while thus ignorant that Jesus would be manifested, and the subordinate office which he himself discharged in his baptism by water.

Verses 32-34 may be a continuation of the preceding testimony, but, as they are separated by the first words of verse thirty-two, they are perhaps rather to be taken as another cognate witness. They differ from the preceding by giving the ground of John's new teaching and confidence, in the visible descent of the Spirit like a dove

Less. II.] Two Days: John's Last and Christ's First 15

on Jesus at His baptism, and its abiding on Him. A Divine message, how or when received we know not, had set John to look for this sign. The abiding is as much a part of it as the descent, for both facts express in visible symbol the Divine operation which fitted the manhood of Jesus for His Messianic work. The Spirit came down, peaceful, tender, upon Him, and abode in Him—not being given by measure, nor at moments of special illumination or power, but in indissoluble union with that pure and perfect manhood, which alone of all men was capable of such perfect reception of the Spirit of God. And the reception of the Spirit by Jesus, in such fashion and measure, is the reason why He is able to "baptize in the Holy Spirit." John gathers all into one great saying, which sums up and concludes his own ministry, and ushers, as it were, the Greater than he on to the scene. For himself, he has seen and borne witness. His work is done. For that other, He is, in the highest sense of that great title, "the Son of God." How much had to be suffered and learned before Christ's disciples could fathom John's words! That clear vision was clouded to him, and still more to them, and did not shine to be no more dimmed till the empty grave and the parting on Olivet had "declared Him to be the Son of God, with power over the Spirit of holiness."

Verses 35-42 tell the events of that fateful "morrow," the first day of Christ's ministry. They fall into two parts,—how Jesus drew two souls to Himself, and how these immediately drew others to Him. John's repeated proclamation was a direct invitation to his disciples to transfer their allegiance to the new Teacher, and the obedience of the two was their deliberate acceptance of Him. The unnamed one was, no doubt, the evangelist himself. Would any other writer have had a motive for omitting one of the two names? Deeply interesting is the frequent use of the name of "the Lamb" in the Apocalypse, if we remember that it was the name which, long before Patmos, on that never-to-be-forgotten day by the fords of the Jordan, had first directed the young fisherman to Jesus. Well for us if our latest faith is but the deepening of our earliest thoughts of that Lord!

The two were following Jesus, as it were, by stealth, when He "turned," as He ever does, to convert secret into open discipleship, and to assure us that He knows unspoken desires. The first words which He speaks are His question to us all, "What seek ye?" He would have us make clear to ourselves what is our aim and true quest in life. He would have us search our hearts to ascertain what we desire from Him, and what we think that He can do for us. The knowledge of our own motives and conceptions of Him and His work underlies all profitable resort to Him; and His question is a veiled promise that the measure of our desires will be the measure of His gifts. Note that His question is "What?" not "Whom?" and that the two are not to be put off with a thing, but seek a person. "Where dwellest Thou?" means "We seek Thee, and to be permanently with Thee." If we can answer Jesus so, we shall be led by Him to secret, sweet converse, and know, as John learned to do, the depth of the word used slightly at first; for we shall "abide" with and in Him.

Jesus' second word is as universal and deep as His

first. "Come and see" is His invitation to us all, and it means that faith must precede experience, and also it promises that experience shall certainly and blessedly follow faith. Note the verbal repetition of the words of invitation in the narrative of what the two did. Obedience was precise, immediate, and it was rewarded according to promise. If our deeds accurately repeat Christ's commands, and we fully respond to His invitations, He will fully accomplish all hopes held out by Him, and will give us more than we dreamed; for the disciples but asked "where" He dwelt, and they not only saw that, but abode there themselves.

No word tells what passed in that sacred interview, begun, as it would seem, in the morning hours, and lasting long. The personal revelation of Jesus, His words and self, bound them to Him for ever. They called Him Teacher before He had spoken to them, but before He ceased to speak they were ready to confess Him to be the Messiah; and from that confession John, at least, never flinched. The attractive force in Christianity is Christ Himself. If we gain a glimpse of Him as He really is, and know what we really seek, we shall be drawn to His service. Personal experience is the best evidence of His divinity.

The Christian Church was founded that day. It began with two members. Their first impulse was to impart their treasure. Observe how the next step is told. Andrew's action is mentioned in such terms as to suggest an unmentioned similar action by the other; for if there were a "first" finding "his own" brother, there was probably a second finding of somebody else's brother. It is extremely improbable that when Andrew brought

Simon to Jesus, John came back unaccompanied by James. But, however that may be, the natural impulse of every true disciple of Christ is here beautifully illustrated. To bring others to Jesus will spontaneously suggest itself to us, if we have found Him for ourselves. The natural craving to utter conviction, the sense of loyalty to Christ and of obligation from brotherhood, will operate to that end. The word "shut up in our hearts" will burn there like a fire, till we become weary of forbearing. If we know nothing of such necessity laid on us from possessing the Gospel, we had better ask ourselves whether we have any firm grasp of it.

The true weapon for us is here shown us. Andrew did not begin to argue with Simon, or to submit to him a few considerations tending to show the reasonableness of Christianity, or the correspondence of the character of Jesus with prophetic or rabbinic teaching. He did not scold or threaten, and he was not in the least eloquent, or poetic, or profound; but he brought his own experience in lieu of any other persuasive, "We have found the Messiah." That is the best thing any of us can say, if we would draw men to Jesus. Nothing can refute "Whereas I was blind, now I see," and not much can resist it. The limits of our work are also here. "He brought him to Jesus." That is all we can do. If we can get a man to come into direct relations with the Lord, that Lord will do the rest.

Christ's treatment of Peter is significant. Christ reads his old character and self; for whether His naming him is supernatural knowledge or not, it implies, and is meant to claim, complete knowledge. He sets in sharp contrast the present and the future of the man,—"Thou art," "Thou shalt be." If the new name be meant to prophesy character, it is a promise that the natural impulsiveness and fitfulness shall be changed into solid steadfastness. If it be intended to set forth office, it is a prophecy that he shall be used for a foundation-stone of the new building of the Church. In either meaning, it at once reveals Christ's knowledge of present and future, and establishes His authority. The imposition of a name was an act of superiority, a designation to office, and a gift of capacity. If we come to Jesus, He will receive us, knowing us altogether in all the weakness of our old selves, and will write upon us a new name, changing by degrees our weakness into calm strength, and haply using us for high service, but, at all events, appointing us such tasks as we can do for and by Him.

Simon took many years and trials to grow up to be Peter, but his destination was disclosed at first. We know that Christ's servants are meant to be clothed with His likeness. Let us "put off the old man and be renewed in the spirit of our minds" first, and then, by daily efforts, "put on the new man," which is our destined attire.

LESSON III

The First Ray of the Glory

St. John ii. 1-11

1. "And the third day there was a marriage in Cana of Galilee; and the mother of Jesus was there:
2. And both Jesus was called, and His disciples, to the marriage.
3. And when they wanted wine, the mother of Jesus saith unto Him, They have no wine.
4. Jesus saith unto her, Woman, what have I to do with thee? Mine hour is not yet come.
5. His mother saith unto the servants, Whatsoever He saith unto you, do it.
6. And there were set there six waterpots of stone, after the manner of the purifying of the Jews, containing two or three firkins apiece.
7. Jesus saith unto them, Fill the waterpots with water. And they filled them up to the brim.
8. And He saith unto them, Draw out now, and bear unto the governor of the feast. And they bare it.
9. When the ruler of the feast had tasted the water that was made wine, and knew not whence it was: (but the servants which drew the water knew;) the governor of the feast called the bridegroom,
10. And saith unto him, Every man at the beginning doth set forth good wine; and when men have well drunk, then that which is worse: but thou hast kept the good wine until now.
11. This beginning of miracles did Jesus in Cana of Galilee, and manifested forth His glory; and His disciples believed on Him."

THIS Gospel records just seven miracles before the resurrection, and it calls them all "signs," or symbolic acts revealing spiritual truth through material things. The eleventh verse gives the point of view from which John regards them, as being manifestations of the "glory as of the only-begotten" Son. They are the sevenfold beams into which that white light is separated. This first of them is, by its place in the series, especially significant. The narrative is vivid, and charged with minute details which speak of an eye-witness, and of communications from Mary, made perhaps in the days when John "took her unto his own home." It tells the preliminaries of the sign, the sign itself, and the effects of the sign.

I. Cana was the home of Nathanael, whose connection with it may possibly have been the reason why Jesus and His six disciples went there. Mary appears to have preceded them, and the invitation to them to have followed their arrival. "The third day" is counted from that when Philip and Nathanael were called, as the distance from John's place of baptizing requires. The addition of so many guests might naturally make supplies run short, and lead Mary to appeal to Jesus, as the cause of the deficiency, to suggest some way of making it good. Her intimation is more than an intimation. It is a request.

The whole incident is best understood by supposing that Mary recognised in Him, not only her Son, but her Lord, however incomplete her faith. That explains her unspoken hope, His answer, and the else unaccountable effect of it on her as shown in her instructions to the servants. She tells the need and leaves Him to deal with it. True prayer makes known wants, in humble confidence that to tell them is sufficient, and submissively refrains from prescribing a course to Him. To speak the need, be it great or small, and to be silent about the way of filling it, becomes those who trust His wise and mighty love.

It need scarcely be said that no trace of sternness or rebuke is in Christ's reply; but while "woman" is respectful and affectionate, the substance of His words gives emphasis to His independence, and declares that, now that He has begun His public work, the old days of "subjection" are ended. Their ways diverge, and henceforward He must be guided by His own consciousness of fitting seasons for His working. Such a declaration implies Mary's knowledge of His mission, and that knowledge is still more inevitably implied in her words to the servants. She still trusts to Him, and so implicitly that she leaves everything to His disposal, and bespeaks obedience for whatever He directs. Christ's delays should but strengthen faith and submission.

No note of time gives the space between Christ's answer and the miracle. It cannot have been long, but He discerned some change in conditions, either material or moral, which in a brief space made much change. Possibly He waited for the deficiency to be apparent to the disciples. Possibly He waited for the voice of His heavenly Father, as well as of His earthly mother. But, at all events, He knew that the right time had come. His clock is not set by ours, and the beats that bring the striking of His hour are not moments, but spiritual conditions.

II. The miracle is next told, and that in very remarkable fashion. There is not a word about the method, nor even a statement that the miracle was wrought. We are told what preceded and followed, but itself is shrouded in silence. The servants fill the waterpots, then "Draw out now," and they draw, and carry to the superintendent of the revels. We cannot even tell where the miracle came in, or how far it extended. Was all the water in these six great vessels, probably some fifty gallons, changed into wine, or was the change effected as the portion required was drawn, and on that portion only? It is impossible to say. The conspicuous feature of the miracle is the entire absence of material means. Sometimes our Lord employed material vehicles, as clay, or spittle, or the touch of His hand; sometimes He wrought by a word. But here there is not even a word. His will silently works with sovereign power on matter which is plastic, as if touched. It is not even "He spake, and it was done," but, more wonderful than even that, He silently willed, and the "conscious water knew its Lord, and blushed." In this beginning of miracles, then, Jesus manifested forth His glory as Creator and Sustainer of all things, without whom was not anything made, and by whom all things consist and change.

III. The results of the miracle are twofold. The ruler of the feast, ignorant of the miracle, unconsciously attests its reality and completeness; the glory manifested in it deepens the faith of the disciples.

The ruler's half-jesting speech compliments the bridegroom's cellar at the expense of his prudence, and, in its intention, is simply a suggestion that he is wasting his best wine in producing it when palates are less sensitive than at the beginning of the entertainment. But it suggests a higher thought. Christ keeps His best till last, whereas the world gives its best first; and, when palates are dulled and appetite diminished, "then that which is worse." How tragically true that is! In many lives the early days of hope and vigour, when all was fresh and wondrous, contrast miserably with the dreary close, when habit and failing strength have taken the edge off all delights of sense; and memory, like a lengthening chain, is dragged along, and, with memory, regrets and remorse. In the weariness and monotony of toilsome middle life, and in the deepening shadows of advancing and solitary old age, worldly men have to drink the dregs of the once foaming cup, which "at the last biteth like a serpent." But Jesus keeps the best for the end. No time can cloy His gifts, but advancing years make them more precious and necessary. In His service, "better is the end of a thing than the beginning thereof." And when life is over here, and we pass into the heavens, this word of the ruler at the humble feast will serve to express our thankful surprise at finding all so much better than our highest hopes and sweetest experiences. "Thou hast kept the good wine until now."

"The best is yet to be,
The last of life, for which the first was planned."

The wider significance of the sign is given in the eleventh verse. It was a manifestation of Christ's glory, and thereby it was the occasion of new faith to the disciples. The light was His, and yet the Father's. The mystery of His being is that His self-revelation was at once "the effulgence of" the Father's "glory," and of His own, as the eternal Light and only-begotten Son. That manifestation (one of John's favourite words) led susceptible hearts to new, deeper faith. It was a sign for those who were already disciples, and had no recorded effect on others. Not only the miraculous fact, but the whole revelation of Christ in the incident, is meant. We have already seen that it "manifested forth His glory" as being a creative act; but there are other gleams from it, which reveal other and gracious aspects of our Lord's character and work.

It is not without meaning that Jesus began His work by sanctioning and hallowing common, and especially family, life. What a contrast there is between the simple gladness of the rustic wedding and the temptation in the wilderness, from which Jesus had just come! What a contrast between the sublime heights of the prologue and this opening scene of the ministry! What a contrast between the rigid, ascetic forerunner and this Son of Man! How unlike the anticipations of the disciples, who would be all tingling with expectation of the first exhibition of His Messiahship! Surely the fact that His first act was to hallow marriage and family life has opened a fountain of sacred blessing. So He breaks down that wicked division of life into sacred and secular which has damaged both parts so much. So He teaches that the sphere of religion is this world, not only another. So He claims as the subjects of His sanctifying power every relation of manhood. So He says at the beginning of His career, "I am a man, and nothing that belongs to manhood do I reckon foreign to Myself." Where He has trod is hallowed ground.

The participation of the prince in the festivities of his people dignifies these. Our King has sat at a wedding feast, and the memory of His presence there adds a new sacredness to the sacredest, and a new sweetness to the sweetest, of human ties. The consecration of His presence, like some pungent and perennial perfume, lingers yet in the else scentless air of daily life. "Sanctity" is not "singularity." We need not withdraw from any region of activity or interest for affection or intellect, in order to develop the whitest saintliness. Christ's saints are to be "in the world, not of it," like their Master, who went from the wilderness and its fearful conflicts to begin His work amid the homely rejoicings of a village wedding.

Further, He manifested His glory as the ennobler and heightener of earthly joys. That may be taken, with a possibly permissible play of fancy, as a lesson suggested, if not as a meaning intended, by the change of water into wine. The latter is, in the Old Testament especially, a symbol of gladness. The Man of Sorrows brings the gift of joy. To make men glad is an object not unworthy of Him. If we may so say, it was worth His while to come from heaven and agonise and die, that He might pour everlasting and pure joy into weary and sad hearts.

We are so much accustomed to draw joys from ignoble sources, that in most of them there is a trace of something not altogether creditable or lofty, and hence we often fail to estimate rightly the importance of joy as an element in Christian life. But Christ came to give the oil of joy for mourning, and He does so in part by transforming the less potent and invigorating draughts from earthen waterpots into the new wine of the kingdom. The commonest joys, if only they are not foul and sinful, are capable of this transformation. If we bring them to Jesus, and are "glad in the Lord," He will ennoble them, and they will tend to ennoble us. A taper plunged into a jar of oxygen blazes more brightly. Without Christ's presence, earth's joys at their best and brightest are like some fair landscape in shadow. When He comes to hallow them—as He always does when He is invited—they are like the same scene when the sun blazes out on it, flashes from every bend of the rippling river, brings beauty into shady corners, opens the flowers, and sets all the birds singing in the sky. Joys on which He can let the sunshine of His smile fall will be bettered and prolonged thereby; joys on which He cannot, are not for His servants to meddle with. If we cannot make the sign of the cross over our mirth, and ask Him to bless it, we had better be sorrowful than glad. If we keep Him out of our mirth, "the end of that mirth is heaviness," however jubilant may be its beginning.

But Christ can not only change the water of human joy into the wine of heavenly gladness, but He can drop an elixir into the cups of sorrow, and change them into cups of blessing and salvation. One drop of that potent influence can sweeten the bitterest draught, even though many a tear has fallen into it. He can make Marah into Elim, and can calm sorrow into a willing acquiescence not wholly unlike happiness. Christian sorrow has a sister's likeness to Christian joy, though complexion and dress be different. Jesus will repeat "this beginning of miracles" in every sad heart that trusts to Him.

Where He is invited as a guest, He brings richer provision than was there before. No man is the poorer by asking Him to accept what He can give. They who bid Him to sup with them shall sup with Him. He supplies the deficiencies of earthly stores. The gifts He gives do not perish with the using. The more we take, the more we have. The largest waterpots will run dry at last; but Christ will give us a fountain within springing unto life eternal, and when the world's cups are empty He will satisfy the blessed thirst of every spirit which longs for Him and His gifts.

LESSON IV

"How Can these Things be?"

St. John iii. 1-17

1. "There was a man of the Pharisees, named Nicodemus, a ruler of the Jews:

2. The same came to Jesus by night, and said unto Him, Rabbi, we know that Thou art a teacher come from God: for no man can do these miracles that Thou doest, except God be with him.

3. Jesus answered and said unto him, Verily, verily, I say unto thee, Except a man be born again, he cannot see the kingdom of God.

4. Nicodemus saith unto Him, How can a man be born when he is old? can he enter the second time into his mother's womb, and be born?

5. Jesus answered, Verily, verily, I say unto thee, Except a man be born of water and of the Spirit, he cannot enter into the kingdom of God.

6. That which is born of the flesh is flesh; and that which is born of the Spirit is spirit.

7. Marvel not that I said unto thee, Ye must be born again.

8. The wind bloweth where it listeth, and thou hearest the sound thereof, but canst not tell whence it cometh, and whither it goeth: so is every one that is born of the Spirit.

9. Nicodemus answered and said unto Him, How can these things be?

10. Jesus answered and said unto him, Art thou a master of Israel, and knowest not these things?

11. Verily, verily, I say unto thee, We speak that we do know, and testify that we have seen; and ye receive not our witness.

12. If I have told you earthly things, and ye believe not, how shall ye believe, if I tell you of heavenly things?

13. And no man hath ascended up to heaven, but He that came down from heaven, even the Son of man which is in heaven.

14. And as Moses lifted up the serpent in the wilderness, even so must the Son of man be lifted up:

15. That whosoever believeth in Him should not perish, but have eternal life.

16. For God so loved the world, that He gave His only begotten Son, that whosoever believeth in Him should not perish, but have everlasting life.

17. For God sent not His Son into the world to condemn the world; but that the world through Him might be saved."

THE designation of Nicodemus as "a man of the Pharisees" connects the narrative with the preceding words, and presents it as an instance of our Lord's discernment of character and motives, even when these were unexpressed and dimly seen by the man himself. He knew Nicodemus better than Nicodemus did, and spoke to his unspoken thoughts. He "committed Himself" to this "man" as seeing what was in him. This wonderful disclosure of the very heart of the gospel, made thus early and to a ruler, can only be touched here in the slightest fashion. Volumes would not exhaust it, but it must suffice to try to grasp its main sequence of thought. In general, we may regard it as Christ's way of educating a man who was ready to recognise Him as a teacher to a fuller perception of what was needed for discipleship, and to a loftier conception of His nature and work. The utterances of Nicodemus divide the whole into three parts.

I. We have the imperfect confession and its reception (vers. 1-3). The nocturnal visit looks like timidity, or, at least, a wish for secrecy and non-committal. The acknowledgment by Nicodemus is made in the name of others. Possibly he was sent by some of his colleagues who shared his conviction, and wished further information as to the programme of this new claimant of Messiahship, or he may have been speaking the general conclusion of the Sanhedrim. If so, they stifled their first clear convictions, and afterwards gave the lie to this confession. Those who said "We know that Thou art a teacher come from God" were not subsequently ashamed to say, with equal confidence and arrogance, "We know that this Man is a sinner," and "we know not from whence He is." Light resisted is quenched. Wilful ignorance calling itself knowledge binds sin on men.

There is an unpleasant tone of superiority, and almost of patronage, in Nicodemus' testimonial. He condescends to recognise in Jesus a "teacher," and calls Him "Rabbi," though He had not graduated in the schools. "From God" is put emphatically first, as if to signalise the irregular inspiration of Jesus; and the prominence given to "we know" implies the speaker's consciousness of the value of such a certificate to this undistinguished teacher. But Nicodemus' error was mainly in his inadequate conception of Christ's nature and work. If we think of Jesus but as a teacher, even if we admit His miracles as attesting God's presence with Him, His true nature and kingdom are hid from our eyes. All merely humanitarian conceptions of Him are here set aside by His own hand, as unworthy of Him and impotent for us.

Whom did Nicodemus mean to convince by his argument about miracles? It was singularly unnecessary as addressed to Jesus, but its introduction suggests that the speaker is reassuring his own somewhat shaky faith, which found difficulty in admitting that a Galilean peasant was a God-made rabbi. He has not said a word about what he came for, and we can only infer it from Christ's answer, which, as so often, replies to thoughts rather than words. He wishes to know more of whether Jesus claims to be the Messiah, and means to carry out the Jewish idea of Messiah's kingdom, which John had shadowed.

Our Lord's answer glances at his "except," and then grapples directly with his unspoken thought, and tells him that the kingdom of God is not brought into being through teachers, but requires, as the condition of even beholding it, an entirely new beginning of life. There must be new eyes for new seeing, and new seeing for this new order of things, the kingdom of God. That principle, which will be further developed in the sequel, sweeps away the idea that the bringer of the kingdom is merely to be either a school-trained rabbi or a God-sent teacher. Something infinitely more and altogether different from that is wanted. Human nature does not require culture, but a new life. If Jesus is but a teacher, He is but one of the long series whose teachings have failed to arrest evil or bring the golden age. This generation, with its confidence in the ennobling and purifying effect of education, needs this truth as much as Nicodemus did.

II. Nicodemus' question is not so foolish as it is often supposed to be. Its second part shows that he recognised the impossibility of the expression "born again" being literally understood; and its first member asks what, in view of that plain impossibility, is the process intended. One does not see what better question he could have asked. The cautions founded upon its supposed inappropriateness, to the effect that we should beware of putting away truths because we do not understand the manner of their being, seem beside the mark. Was not this question the very one which Jesus desired to evoke? His answer does not deal with it as either absurd or improper, but as the very thing for which He had been waiting. That answer (vers. 5-8) is an explanation of the manner and an enforcement of the necessity of this new birth. In the fifth verse both of these thoughts are stated, and rested on the sole authority of Jesus.

The duplicated "verily," which is peculiar to this Gospel, at once claims absolute authority for the teacher, attests the importance of the lesson, and calls for our best attention. We are bound to take His statements on His bare word. What is arrogant presumption in a human teacher is consistent with meekness in Him. The truth thus heralded is all-important. Nicodemus' "how can" is fully answered.

This new life is communicated "by water and Spirit." Whatever be the meaning of the former factor, "water," its omission in the eighth verse shows that it is not on the same level as the latter, "Spirit." It is generally referred to baptism, and, if so, the relation of the two terms is that of symbol and thing symbolised; or, it may be, of cleansing for the past old life, and impartation of the new. But the explanation, which follows the analogy of John the Baptist's phrase "with the Holy Ghost and with fire," taking water to mean simply the purifying energy of the Spirit, is more in accordance with our Lord's absolute silence, till the last of His words, in reference to the rite, and with the omission in verse eight.

The necessity of the new birth is still more strongly affirmed as the condition, not only of perceiving, but of entering into, the kingdom of God. Therein is contained the declaration of the spiritual character of that kingdom, which, however it may be manifested on earth in institutions, is essentially that order of things in which the will of God reigns supreme. The Sanhedrim's dreams, which Nicodemus shared, are shattered by the words. The necessity of this new birth is enforced in the sixth verse by the consideration that, as a stream cannot rise above its source, the child but repeats the elements belonging to the parent. "Flesh," by which is meant the whole of human nature apart from the life-giving Spirit, can but produce flesh. Man cannot find within the limits of his own powers the conditions necessary for entrance into the kingdom. The same law of kinship holds in the higher region. Spiritual birth results in a life like its source. That life, by its spiritual nature, is fit to enter a kingdom which is spiritual. Therefore, these things being so, the stringent demand for a new birth as preliminary to becoming a subject of Messiah's (which is God's) kingdom should cause no wonder.

Mark our Lord's emphatic "ye," corresponding to Nicodemus' "we," but also significantly excepting Himself from the universal need.

A symbol lies ready at hand which may lighten the wonder. The word necessarily translated "wind" in verse eight is that used in the rest of the conversation, as always, for "spirit"; and the operation and effects of the one agent are illustrations of those of the other. The former seems to blow where it listeth, so little do we know even yet of the laws determining its course. It is audible in its effect, though unseen in itself, and its source and its goal are beyond us. Thus free in its working, invisible but manifest in result, coming from hidden depths in God, and passing on to unknown issues, the breath of God is breathed into "flesh," and makes it, too, "spirit." Mark the significance of the apparently irregular comparison attributing all these characteristics, not, as we expect, to the Spirit, but to every one born thereby. The offspring is as the parent. The Christian in his new life has the law of the spirit of life within, and is free thereby. The depths of his hidden life cannot be tracked by fleshly eyes, but its results are manifest. It has its origin in the secrets of Divine love, and its goal is among things which eye hath not seen.

So Jesus answers the question, "How can a man be born when he is old?" A new life, which the Spirit of God will give, is the only possible qualification for entrance into the kingdom of God, either here or in its ultimate perfection. What use would a "teacher" be, if that be so?

III. Nicodemus' third utterance repeats more curtly, and, as it were, wearily, his former question. Christ's answer has a tone of rebuke at first, implying the presence of something wrong, but soon passes to answer with infinite patience what was good in the question, by unfolding the great work which made it possible that "these things" should "be." The conditions of entrance into the kingdom having been laid down, the means of compliance with them are next set forth. The tenth verse has an accent of rebuke, and implies that "these things" —that is, the necessity and reality of a spiritual influence recreating men—were so far taught in the Old Testament that the men whose business was to expound it, and whose boast was that they "knew," should have been familiar with them. Many a psalm (Jer. xxxi. 33; Ezek. xxxvi. 26) taught these truths. Ecclesiastics blind to the vital centre of the revelation which they assume to expound are found in all Churches.

The eleventh verse rebukes Nicodemus on another ground,—that he was putting away strong testimony to the truths in hand. But who are the "we" here associated with Jesus? The best answer is, the little group of disciples, who, however imperfectly, had in some measure accepted Christ's teaching, and begun to know the mysteries of the kingdom. On the one side are the Pharisees, represented by Nicodemus, with his "we know"; on the other, the handful of Christ's followers who could say, "We have seen, and we know," with better right.

The essential distinction of true Christian witnessing is here set forth, in some measure anticipatively, as being the result of personal and immediate knowledge; and John's first words in his Epistle are an echo. The clearness of the witness and the reliableness of its source make the guilt of rejecting the more deep, and the wonder of it the more wonderful and sad. This tenderly condescending "we" makes the presence of some, at least, of the disciples probable; and that would explain the minute fulness of narrative, since, if any were there, John would be.

The twelfth verse warns Nicodemus and us all that the rejection of light given bars the reception of higher light, and saddens the Speaker of it. It may seem strange that the truths just spoken should be called "earthly"; but the strangeness disappears if we remember that that epithet means having their place of manifestation on earth. The new birth is not earthly in the sense of belonging by nature to earth, but it is in that other of being brought about and operating on earth. So it is capable of verification through its effects, and therefore should be easier to receive than the next declaration to be made. A solemn lesson as to the connection between our attitude to the first and second stages of Christ's teaching is wrapped up in these words. If we will not learn *a*, we stand small chance of learning *b*.

The thirteenth verse naturally follows the claim that

Jesus was the trustworthy Revealer of heavenly things. There was a witness to the earthly in which others were united with Him, but in telling the heavenly He stood alone. His sole office therein, and the reliableness of these revelations resting on His word only, depend on that great fact that He came down from heaven, and that, as Son of Man, He is in heaven even while on earth. His pre-existence, incarnation, continual communion with the Father, uniqueness, and, as consequence of all, His right to tell heavenly things, and our obligation to receive them, simply because He has said them, are all included in these few words.

And what are the heavenly things thus solemnly brought to us for our faith? The fact of the mission of the Son of God from the heart of the Father. Of course, the incarnation and the crucifixion are earthly things, in so far as they have their fulfilment on earth; but they are heavenly, inasmuch as all which gives them their value, and distinguishes them from any other birth or death, lies in the heavenly truths unfolded in verses 14-18. The brazen serpent was in the likeness of the cause of the disease. Jesus came in the likeness of sinful flesh. Its elevation was the symbol of the defeat of the evil, and the means of making it conspicuous. Christ was lifted on the cross in order to slay the sin in the likeness of which He, sinless, died. A look brought healing. Faith beholds, and is whole. The shameful elevation of the cross was one stage in the elevation to the throne, and Nicodemus and we are to learn that the victory of the King is in His apparent defeat, and the degradation of the lofty cross the direct path to the height of the throne.

The sacrificial death of Christ on the cross, as in obedience to a necessity ("must") arising from the very nature of God, the great gift of eternal life flowing from Him to us, and the condition on which that gift is ours,—namely, faith in Him,—are the heavenly things which Jesus unfolded to Nicodemus as the full answer to his question of how that new birth could be brought about. Clearly, the knowledge which each man may have of his own character, and the experience which he has of men, confirm the earlier declaration that a radical change, comparable to a new birth, is needful before such a mortal creature can enter into the state of perfect obedience to God's perfect will. As clearly, such a change can only be effected by superhuman—that is, by Divine—power. Then comes the great question, Can and will such a power be put forth; and, if so, where is it, and how may I have it working on me? The second part of this conversation answers these questions. Jesus Christ, the Son of God, the Son of Man, has come from the Father, sent by the Father's love. He has died on the cross for sin-stricken men. The look of faith brings His gifts into our hearts. Eternal life is the life conferred in the new birth. They who believe in His name are born, not of flesh, but of God; and to them He gives the Spirit, which quickens and changes their sinful selves into its own likeness, and gives them authority to become sons of God.

LESSON V

The Thirsty Giver of Living Water

St. John iv. 5-26

5. "Then cometh He to a city of Samaria, which is called Sychar, near to the parcel of ground that Jacob gave to his son Joseph.

6. Now Jacob's well was there. Jesus therefore, being wearied with His journey, sat thus on the well: and it was about the sixth hour.

7. There cometh a woman of Samaria to draw water: Jesus saith unto her, Give Me to drink.

8. (For His disciples were gone away unto the city to buy meat.)

9. Then saith the woman of Samaria unto Him, How is it that Thou, being a Jew, askest drink of me, which am a woman of Samaria? for the Jews have no dealings with the Samaritans.

10. Jesus answered and said unto her, If thou knewest the gift of God, and who it is that saith to thee, Give Me to drink; thou wouldest have asked of Him, and He would have given thee living water.

11. The woman saith unto Him, Sir, Thou hast nothing to draw with, and the well is deep: from whence then hast Thou that living water?

12. Art Thou greater than our father Jacob, which gave us the well, and drank thereof himself, and his children, and his cattle?

13. Jesus answered and said unto her, Whosoever drinketh of this water shall thirst again:

14. But whosoever drinketh of the water that I shall give him shall never thirst; but the water that I shall give him shall be in him a well of water springing up into everlasting life.

15. The woman saith unto Him, Sir, give me this water, that I thirst not, neither come hither to draw.

16. Jesus saith unto her, Go, call thy husband, and come hither.

17. The woman answered and said, I have no husband. Jesus said unto her, Thou hast well said, I have no husband:

18. For thou hast had five husbands; and he whom thou now hast is not thy husband: in that saidst thou truly.

19. The woman saith unto Him, Sir, I perceive that Thou art a prophet.

20. Our fathers worshipped in this mountain; and ye say, that in Jerusalem is the place where men ought to worship.

21. Jesus saith unto her, Woman, believe Me, the hour cometh, when ye shall neither in this mountain, nor yet at Jerusalem, worship the Father.

22. Ye worship ye know not what: we know what we worship: for salvation is of the Jews.

23. But the hour cometh, and now is, when the true worshippers shall worship the Father in spirit and in truth: for the Father seeketh such to worship Him.

24. God is a Spirit: and they that worship Him must worship Him in spirit and in truth.

25. The woman saith unto Him, I know that Messias cometh, which is called Christ: when He is come, He will tell us all things.

26. Jesus saith unto her, I that speak unto thee am He."

THERE are seven sayings of our Lord in this conversation, which may be regarded as the seven rounds of a ladder whose foot is on earth and its top in heaven. The first is the request "Give Me to drink," which reveals a true manhood participant of physical need and dependent on help. The last is the full revelation of His dignity in "I that speak unto thee am He." How wide the distance between these two! The path from the valley to the height, and the reasons for making a Samaritan woman the recipient of so clear a revelation of the truth veiled from His own people, will appear in studying the narrative. Observe that in the earlier part of the conversation Jesus takes the initiative and the woman answers, while in the latter, after her conscience has been roused, the parts are reversed. The passive recipient becomes the active inquirer.

We must leave all topography and picturesque treatment to others, and simply note the first step in the ladder. Try to see with the woman's eyes a travel-worn

Jew sitting alone by the well, and to hear with her ears the request for a draught of water, which He evidently sorely needed. Her question (probably put while she was giving the boon asked for) is the simple expression of wonder, with a little dash of rustic raillery in it, as who should say, "Oh, then, a thirsty Jew is not quite so proud as he would be if He did not want anything! You can speak to a Samaritan, and that a woman, when she can help you." Her wonder would have been greater if she had known the deepest answer to her question, His elevation above all national distinctions and equal kinship to every human soul.

But, if we look at this scene with eyes enlightened by fuller knowledge, how wonderful and precious it is, as one pathetic evidence of the true humanity and humiliation of our Lord! He whose goings forth were of old sat, a weary traveller, too tired to go with the disciples to buy food, which He needed. The blazing sun, His creature, made Him thirst who stills the cravings of souls. Our question should be, "How is it that Thou, being the Son of God, needest and askest drink of one of us?" The answer carries us deep into the mysteries of God and the heart of the gospel.

The second step (vers. 10-12) is like a partial opening of a giving hand to show a corner of the gift lying in it, which is met by a half-bewildered answer, through which appears a dawning sense of some deeper meaning than the speaker has grasped. Our Lord does not yet afford any clear indication of the nature of the gift, but simply seeks to awaken a sense of great possibilities to be had for the asking. He links His words on to the woman's expressed wonder that He, being what she sees

Him, should cross the barrier to her. If she knew who He, the "Jew," was, a deeper wonder would open to her, and it would be she who would sue to Him. "The gift of God" is not defined, but the very generality of the phrase stirs desires. It is perhaps best left in that generality, as here meaning all that God gives through Christ.

Two things then are pointed out, in which He would have her feel her ignorance,—the gift of God, and the true nature of Him, the Giver. If men rightly understood what God wishes to give them, the knowledge could not but kindle desire. If they understood it was a gift, they would know that asking was the way to get it. If they knew that Christ gave God's gift, they would know to ask Him. That "if thou knewest" is, on Christ's lips, a lament as well as a palliation. This woman's ignorance was innocent. Ours is not. But the knowledge here meant is more than intellectual apprehension; for, alas! it is possible to know in that way both of these subjects, and to have no motions of desire towards them. Not only will real knowledge produce desire, but every desire addressed to Jesus will be answered. The sequence is certain. "Know," "ask," "have," are links soldered fast together.

What is the "living water"? Of course, the form of the symbol has reference to the occasion of the whole conversation. But the occurrence of the same metaphor in the words to Nicodemus as to "water and the Spirit," and again in the great scene in the temple court (John vii. 37), suggests that the emblem is here used for the gift of the Holy Spirit. If so, the subsequent teaching of the nature of true worship is based on the promise in this earlier part of the conversation, and a new link between the parts is brought to light. But whatever the meaning may be, there is no explanation of it at this stage. Enough if now some longing for the unknown precious gift and some dawnings of trust in its Giver begin to move in the woman.

Her reply indicates growing seriousness and incipient awe. She addresses Jesus with a title of respect, and her question, pointing out the physical impossibility, is like Nicodemus' parallel one, the first trace of perception that more is meant than water. Her second question lays hold of Christ's hint of concealed greatness; and while it puts emphasis on "Thou,"—a wearied, thirsty, solitary wayfarer,—and magnifies, with a touch of national jealousy, " our father Jacob," whom she calls, with distinct reference to Christ's promise to give, the "giver" of " the well," there is a tone of reverence in it which seems to invite fuller disclosure. Thus far Christ's dealing has told as He desired.

The next step (vers. 13-15) is a fuller explanation of the gift, answered by asking which, however imperfect, is not in vain. Water gives temporary relief to thirst, and so all creatural delights and goods allay desires for a space only. They fail in permanence because they are external. If men are ever to cease to thirst, they must have an inward fountain. Nothing outside of me can permanently still my nature. Jesus does not define His gift, but tells its blessed effects. He has something to give which will pass into the spirit, and, there abiding, will not only quench a moment's thirst, but will be a self-reproducing fountain,—not merely like water in a cup or even in Jacob's well, but "leaping up" towards and reaching to the eternal life from which it came. A satisfying gift, an inward gift, a satisfying inward gift, which is itself an active principle and the quickener of action where it dwells, and which ever tends towards the perfect consummation of eternal life,—what can this gift be but that Spirit which He gives, and which is in us the ground of all enduring blessedness, the spring of all glad energy, the inspirer of all reachings of heart and mind towards the perfect life, of which it is the earnest? The great words in the seventh chapter, already referred to, are the best commentary on this saying.

The woman's wonder has deepened into awe, and her glimmering suspicions of something great in this "Jew" pass into longings to possess this gift; and her petition, though it be spoken as in twilight, bears witness that new desires are beginning. She does not understand, but she feels that somehow this Stranger can give her the cure of two evils, unsatisfied thirst and weary toil, the latter being pathetically expressed in the Revised Version's "come all the way hither." Even the dimmest perception of His gift, which is strong enough to wing a prayer to Him, is strong enough to bring an answer. Even the desire to have earthly necessities supplied and earthly toil alleviated is acceptable to Him.

The next step (vers. 16, 17) is the unexpected home-thrust at her sin and the roused conscience. No explanation of the startling suddenness of this address is sufficient, if it supposes that Jesus did not know her circumstances, or did not mean it as an assault on her conscience. What other reason could there be for breaking in on the flow of the conversation? The lesson taught by this sudden demand is that the consciousness of sin

The Thirsty Giver of Living Water

must be evoked, and penitence precede the reception of Christ's gift. The direct way to answer the woman's prayer is to rouse her conscience.

The woman's answer proves that she is under the spell of Christ's influence. There is shame in its brevity, but also the need to tell Him the shameful truth. Perhaps there may be also a shade of doubt whether He could have the mysterious power she was beginning to think He had, since He seemed to err. Did she half think that she had found Him tripping? If so, the next step sets her right.

It is (vers. 17, 18) the full disclosure of her sin and the full recognition of His prophetic authority. "He knew all men" (John ii. 24), and His minute knowledge of the foul details drove home the conviction that He was "a prophet." She has got nearer the true conception than Nicodemus, with his cold statement of a reasoned conviction. A quickened conscience is a good teacher. She does not resent the Stranger's intrusion into her past, nor make excuses, but, as it were, falls in a heap at His feet, utterly abject before Him. They are not beyond hope who are within reach of conviction of sin. From this point onward the woman takes the initiative, and Christ answers. That is a sign of growing interest and earnestness.

So the next step (vers. 20-24) is her reference of the fundamental question between her people and His to His prophetic authority. The supposition that her question was only a diversion, to get away from further allusions to her life, is inconsistent both with her previous attitude of reverence and awe and with the tone of Christ's answer. The question raised by her divided the two peoples, was important, and had evidently been seriously thought of by her. She must have been profoundly impressed by Jesus, to think of asking Him, "being a Jew," to decide it for her. She all but offers, in asking His judgment, to become a proselyte. But her notions are those of formal worshippers, to whom the place made worship acceptable, and who were more concerned about the *where* than the *how* or the *whom*. She leaves out the name of the object of worship, as if that were less important than the locality.

Our Lord's great answer lifts her high above half-pagan notions. It deals with a prospect for the future and a privilege for the present. At some hour, which is yet to come and will come, the religion of sacred places will melt away, with all its antagonisms, in a worship which will be universal because it is filial. When that hour strikes, Gerizim and Jerusalem will equally be forsaken shrines. The fatherhood of God is the great truth which Jesus proclaims as determining the externals of worship.

But He also answers the question as to the relative worth of Samaritan and Jewish worship. The difference does not lie in the place of worship, but in the knowledge of the worshippers. The Samaritans had cut themselves off from God's progressive revelation of Himself in Israel, and therefore their worship was of an unknown somewhat. The God to whom men attain by any other path than that of accepting His historical revelation of Himself, is a dim and colourless abstraction, a peradventure, an object of fear or hope, as may be, but not of knowledge. Only they who accept and profit by that historical revelation can be said to "know what they worship."

The reason for this knowledge of the object of worship is that, by God's appointment, "the [promised] salvation" was to proceed from the Jews, which implies a process of revelation among them. The woman's question is thus answered, the true prerogative of Israel set forth, even while the universal destination of that salvation is asserted, and the fading away of all national pre-eminence and local sanctity in the universal worship of the Father foretold.

But the present has its privilege and its duty, as well as the future its glorious, wide prospect. "The hour now is." Because Jesus has come, *it* has come. His coming is the revelation of the Father, and is the Father's seeking for true worshippers. Such words, though partially understood, would lead the woman to feel more and more the mysterious greatness of the Speaker, and would sound as inviting her to become such a worshipper. The true sanctuary is the worshipper's "spirit," that higher part or aspect of human nature which is capable of communion with God. Worship in spirit is possible only on the basis of Christ's work. It leaves all questions of externals at the foot of the mountain. But that communion in spirit with the Divine Spirit is to be also "in truth." A true, though not full, knowledge is possible on the basis of Christ's revelation, which gives the substance of Jewish ritual shadows and the reality which heathenism had overlaid with errors. True ideas and right feelings are both drawn from Him.

The last step (vers. 25, 26) is the woman's Messianic hope and Christ's full disclosure of Himself. The alien, heretical Samaritan has a loftier ideal of Messiah than the orthodox Jew. She thinks of a perfect Enlightener;

he thought of a temporal prince. The heretic may have in some respects a higher ideal than the orthodox whose orthodoxy is stiffened into form. This soul, though stained with fleshly lusts, and groping in much darkness, was ready to hail Messiah; and that for the sake of His revealing power, and not for lower gifts.

Therefore Jesus at last throws back the cloak, of which He had let a fold or two be blown aside, and stands confessed in His full sovereign authority. Docile reception of partial knowledge, and desire for its increase, are ever rewarded. "Whosoever hath, to him shall be given." An alien woman receives the full-orbed truth which was hidden from rabbis and Pharisees. That Christ who comes to give the Spirit which is the water of life, and to reveal the Father, and to make worship in spirit and truth possible for the humblest, will hold familiar converse with outcasts and sinners. The initial wonder of His speaking to an alien pales before the stupendous wonder that the eternal Word becomes flesh and talks, with human lips and Divine condescension, with us.

LESSON VI

The Life-Giver and Judge

ST. JOHN v. 17-30

17. "But Jesus answered them, My Father worketh hitherto, and I work.

18. Therefore the Jews sought the more to kill Him, because He not only had broken the Sabbath, but said also that God was His Father, making Himself equal with God.

19. Then answered Jesus and said unto them, Verily, verily, I say unto you, The Son can do nothing of Himself, but what He seeth the Father do: for what things soever He doeth, these also doeth the Son likewise.

20. For the Father loveth the Son, and showeth Him all things that Himself doeth: and He will show Him greater works than these, that ye may marvel.

21. For as the Father raiseth up the dead, and quickeneth them; even so the Son quickeneth whom He will.

22. For the Father judgeth no man, but hath committed all judgment unto the Son.

23. That all men should honour the Son, even as they honour the Father. He that honoureth not the Son honoureth not the Father which hath sent Him.

24. Verily, verily, I say unto you, He that heareth My word, and believeth on Him that sent Me, hath everlasting life, and shall not come into condemnation; but is passed from death unto life.

25. Verily, verily, I say unto you, The hour is coming, and now is, when the dead shall hear the voice of the Son of God: and they that hear shall live.

26. For as the Father hath life in Himself; so hath He given to the Son to have life in Himself;

27. And hath given Him authority to execute judgment also, because He is the Son of man.

28. Marvel not at this: for the hour is coming, in the which all that are in the graves shall hear His voice,

29. And shall come forth; they that have done good, unto the resurrection of life; and they that have done evil, unto the resurrection of damnation.

30. I can of Mine own self do nothing: as I hear, I judge: and My judgment is just; because I seek not Mine own will, but the will of the Father which hath sent Me."

IT was a strange state of mind to admit that Jesus "did these things,"—namely, miracles,—and yet to take offence that it was "on the Sabbath day." Our Lord's wonderful answer to these pedantic formalists made one offence into two. Hatred sometimes divines meanings hidden from love. The Jews were right when they interpreted Him as claiming to be the Son of God in a special sense ("*His own* Father"), and as therein asserting equality with God. That great saying in the seventeenth verse is the germ of all this lesson's remarkable teaching. The Divine rest, which the Sabbath symbolises, is not cessation of action. Both in that preservation which is a continual creation, and in redeeming activity, God unceasingly works. And the Son's work is of the same order and conforms to the same law. The rest of the lesson is Christ's defence of that claim, the greatness of which had thrown His original offence of Sabbath-breaking into the shade. Perhaps we may take the triple "Verily, verily," as marking its stages.

I. Verses 19-23 assert that the work of the Son is absolutely coincident and coextensive with that of the Father, predict still more signal instances of that working of Divine work by the Son, and, as practical consequence of that identity of working, claim identity of reverence for the Son and the Father. Throughout the whole the personality of Jesus is kept subordinate to the exposition of the relation of fatherhood and sonship in its most perfect form. A true son will do as his father does; a true father will lovingly confide his motives and methods to the son. Such ideal perfectness of paternal confidence and filial following, Jesus declares, though without as yet distinctly presenting His own person, to subsist between

Him and God. The tremendous claim is made first negatively, and then positively,—He does nothing of Himself, but everything which God does, He does. So, entire suppression of the human self, clear vision of the working of God, power to do whatever Divine power can do, and to do all these "in like manner," are the claims made here by Jesus. How can His pretensions to be a meek and lowly pattern and religious teacher be sustained in the face of such tremendous assertions, except we believe Him to be Divine? Surely there is no escaping the conclusion that, if He ever said such things, He is either arrogant to the verge of madness, and undeserving of credit as a teacher and of imitation as a pattern, or else He is the Son of God, able to do Divine works, and worthy of Divine honour.

The ground of this absolute correspondence is laid (ver. 20) in the Father's love, which implies perfect communication of purposes and deeds. The words give a glimpse into the eternal depths of Deity, and show there the energy of love and the possibility of communion before creatures were. They claim for the incarnate Son the same unbroken share in the love of the Father and undimmed vision of His work. They marvellously unite lowly subordination and sameness of nature, and however little we can read all their depths, they unmistakably proclaim that He of whom they are true is Divine.

But the communication is further set forth as being gradual and progressive, and "greater works" are yet to be shown and done. The miracles, of which one had occasioned this whole discourse, are here put below the future work, whether of redemption by the cross, or of rule from the throne, or of resurrection and judgment.

The whole of these are unitedly "the work of Christ," of which the single works are parts. Wonder is not the final aim of any of His works, but the beginning of the path which ends in faith. Wonder may breed attention, and attention may recognise the truth which makes the wonderful natural ("Marvel *not*," ver. 28). It rouses the soul, but its worth depends on what the roused soul does next. If it beholds and despises, it wonders and perishes; if it wonderingly beholds and cries "My Lord and my God!" it lives and grows familiar with what was once so strange.

Verses 21 and 22 instance two of these greater works, and give definiteness to the claim of the correspondence of the Son's work with the Father's. He has the Divine power of giving and restoring life, and the awful prerogative of judgment. These two are here stated in their most general form, and in a more developed fashion (as is usual in St. John's Gospel and Epistle) in the subsequent context. It is God who kills and makes alive, and only a Divine person could exercise that power on "whom He will." Others might and could wield it, as mere channels of Divine will; but Jesus was not a mere instrument, but the source of power, when He stopped the bier with "I say unto thee, Arise." That is no contradiction of His preceding disavowal of doing anything of Himself, but is the assurance that His will ever coincided with the Father's, as well as the claim to be Himself the true raiser from the dead, whether the bodily or spiritually dead. Are we listening to a mere man like ourselves? If so, shall we call Him saint, sage, or blasphemer?

The prerogative of judgment is adduced as the ground,

or perhaps rather as the proof, of the other of life-giving; and here for a moment the identity of the action of the Father and the Son seems broken, for the "Father judges no man." But it is still retained in essence; for it is the Father who has given the authority to judge. Again we have to mark the many-sidedness of the ineffable relation of Father and Son, which, when it is presented in human speech, can only be shadowed by apparent opposites, such as occur throughout this context. They are not contradictions, but indications that the full comprehension of the truth which they complimentarily set forth is beyond us. Note, too, the view here given of the Son's work, present as well as future: He is, not merely will be, the Judge. In one aspect He said, "God sent not His Son . . . to judge the world." In another He said, "For judgment I am come into this world."

The purpose of all this communication of Divine powers and prerogatives is next stated, in words which one cannot read without a shudder, unless one accepts them as the utterance of a truly Divine consciousness. Jesus declares that He is meant to receive a universal homage, precisely identical with that rendered to God; and He further dares to assert that to withhold such from Him is to withhold it from God. Yet the claim is the claim of a Son; and, even in making it, though it surely is the most awful that ever came from sane lips, He does not forget His filial subordination.

Can any theory of His nature do justice to both sides of these solemn sayings, except that which sees in Him the Word made flesh, who in the beginning was with God and was God?

II. The second "verily, verily" (ver. 24) further unfolds the bearing of the two great ideas of life-giving and judgment. The personality of Jesus is more prominent ("*My* word"). The conditions on which men receive life and escape judgment are set forth with majestic absoluteness, and all is commended as sufficiently established by nothing more than His bare word. A teacher of a new sort this, who makes the most astounding and awful assertions, and never stops to prove them, but simply says, "I tell you so, and that is enough." What must He have thought of His word, who could thus calmly declare that to accept it, and to trust in Him whom it revealed, secures present possession of eternal life and exemption from judgment? That life is a resurrection; for every one possessing it passes from death into it. The world is a graveyard. It was spoken of to Nicodemus as a birth, here it is a resurrection. The Son "quickens whom He will"; but that will is neither arbitrary as regards men, nor self-asserting as regards the Father. The law of its harmonies with the latter we do not know, but its conditions as to ourselves we do. He wills to quicken all who receive His word. The reception of that word removes its receivers from the incidence of the judgment which follows future resurrection; for the possession of eternal life negatives the need and possibility of judgment; and if Christ's words are daily judging and cleansing us here, and by their light "we judge ourselves, we shall not be judged." These great gifts are present gifts. The eternal life is ours to-day, and the abolition of judgment in all its terrible aspects, while it is active in all its beneficent ones, is the privilege of every believing soul here and now.

III. The third "verily, verily" introduces the full development of these two great ideas, filling up their contents and discriminating their aspects (vers. 25-27). The first broadly marked feature is the clear separation of two stages or epochs of resurrection and judgment,— one present ("the hour cometh, and now is"), one future ("cometh"). Clearly the former refers to the spiritual quickening which has been spoken of in verse twenty-four, as is established by that remarkable limitation, "They that hear shall live," which is only explicable by supposing that "the dead" are those sunk in the death of sin and self, and that, among these, there are the two classes of "some who believed" and "some who believed not." They can exercise choice though they be dead, and, if they will, can be deaf as well as dead. Our Lord's personality is again veiled; and while He spoke of His voice in the former verse, here He speaks of "the voice of the Son of God." The quickening power of that voice is traced (ver. 26) to the Son's possession of "life in Himself,"—a Divine prerogative, which yet, by a bold paradox, is declared to be "given." The two expressions "given" and "in Himself" seem mutually exclusive, and can only be reconciled by the recognition of the mysterious relation of Fatherhood and Sonship in the depths of Deity. That Son, being in Himself possessor of life, can impart it, and does do so to all who hear His voice. The prerogative of judgment necessarily resides where the power of life-giving resides, but is here connected with our Lord's manhood, rather than with His Divine Sonship, as it was in verse 22. It is a Divine office, needing omniscience and other purely Divine attributes, and these are presupposed as included in verse 22; but it is a blessed addition to the thought that the Judge of men must be a man, who knows our frame, not only with the knowledge of a God, but by the experience of a man, and, as Judge no less than as priestly Intercessor, "can have compassion on the ignorant, and on them that are out of the way."

Verses 28 and 29 obviously refer to a future event, the hour of which "comes," but is not "now"; and that event is unmistakably the universal resurrection of the corporeally dead, as is clear from the unambiguous description of its objects, as "all that are in the graves," and from the addition, as compared with verse 24, of "shall come forth"; and, yet more solemnly, from the twofold nature of this resurrection, contrasted with the one blessed result of that former. Life-giving is once more connected with judgment; but now the life given is of such a kind that only a portion of its recipients partake of "the resurrection of life," while others, who also live again, have their resurrection unto "judgment." The true life is the antithesis of the final judgment; and they who hear the voice of Jesus here and now shall not come into that final judgment, while they who hear it not shall at last hear it, and rise to a life which is not life, but judgment.

Verse 30 carries us back to the beginning of this wonderful outpouring of Christ's consciousness. His own personality is now put in the foreground, as if insisting on the application of all these great sayings concerning "the Son" to Himself. But while He thus makes the most awful claims, lowly self-abnegation blends in the most unheard-of manner with these. He declares Himself to be the fountain of life, the Judge of the world, the eternal Son of God, capable of doing all Divine acts; and yet He abjures all independent self-willed activity, and proclaims, in words of which their lowliness and their consciousness of complete and continual conformity with the Father's will are equally unique, that His judgments are always just, because they are always the utterance of the Father's, which He ever hears, because, without the smallest deflection, His human will is conformed and submitted to the Father's. This closing utterance of Christ's self-consciousness is lowly humility in Him. What but the very insanity of self-righteousness and fancied infallibility would it be in any other man that ever lived?

LESSON VII

Bread Enough, and to Spare

St. John vi. 1-14

1. "After these things Jesus went over the sea of Galilee, which is the sea of Tiberias.
2. And a great multitude followed Him, because they saw His miracles which He did on them that were diseased.
3. And Jesus went up into a mountain, and there He sat with His disciples.
4. And the passover, a feast of the Jews, was nigh.
5. When Jesus then lifted up His eyes, and saw a great company come unto Him, He saith unto Philip, Whence shall we buy bread, that these may eat?
6. And this He said to prove Him: for He Himself knew what He would do.
7. Philip answered Him, Two hundred pennyworth of bread is not sufficient for them, that every one of them may take a little.
8. One of His disciples, Andrew, Simon Peter's brother, saith unto Him,
9. There is a lad here, which hath five barley loaves, and two small fishes: but what are they among so many?
10. And Jesus said, Make the men sit down. Now there was much grass in the place. So the men sat down, in number about five thousand.
11. And Jesus took the loaves; and when He had given thanks, He distributed to the disciples, and the disciples to them that were set down; and likewise of the fishes as much as they would.
12. When they were filled, He said unto His disciples, Gather up the fragments that remain, that nothing be lost.
13. Therefore they gathered them together, and filled twelve baskets with the fragments of the five barley loaves, which remained over and above unto them that had eaten.
14. Then those men, when they had seen the miracle that Jesus did, said, This is of a truth that prophet that should come into the world."

"AFTER these things." What things? Those recorded in the fifth chapter as having occurred in Jerusalem. There must, therefore, be inserted before this narrative a journey from Jerusalem to Galilee; and, if the preceding incidents took place, as is probable, at the Feast of Purim, several weeks had passed in Galilee. Our narrative omits also our Lord's reasons for this retirement to the eastern shores of the lake. John's attention is fixed on the significance of the miracle, as developed in the subsequent discourse on the bread of life, to which it gave occasion, and on its importance as a turning-point in the people's estimate of Jesus, to whom they at first clung with enthusiastic hope, and from whom they departed when the miracle was followed by His "hard sayings" founded on it.

The double name for the lake is an indication that this Gospel was not addressed to Jews familiar with the scene. Its readers were more likely to have known the name of Tiberias than the other. Verse 2 describes vividly not merely the circumstances of that one time, but the habitual environment at that period,—a throng of eager gazers, drawn by curiosity more than by any deeper feelings, who pressed on Jesus, regardless of delicacy or of His need for repose and privacy. Part of the reason for crossing the lake was to avoid these intrusive sight-seers, but they came hurrying after, making their way on foot round the head of the sea, and destroying the seclusion needed both by Him and by the disciples, who had just come back from their trial mission. They had found some quiet spot on the hillside, and there "He sat with His disciples," glad of this breathing-time. The note of time, in verse 4, explains the crowd, and may also hint at the spiritual significance of the feast, which was a truer passover than that in Jerusalem.

The first point to observe is Christ's cheerful giving up of repose and quick sympathetic foresight of men's needs. No impatience disturbs His calm as the vulgar crowd come flocking towards Him. He surrenders the prospect of quiet without a sigh, being ever ready to "please not Himself," and finding His meat in doing the Father's will. Before the mob is at His side, He thinks for them of a want which they had not thought of. They were not hungry yet, and had not troubled themselves about food. But He cared for the careless. His heart foresaw their need, and already knew what He would do to supply it. So is it ever. Before we call, He answers, and prepares to supply necessities as yet unfelt.

The next point is the question asked by conscious power and answered by practical common sense. In the Synoptics, the question of how to get provision is discussed first among the apostles privately at the close of the day. John not only makes it originate with Jesus, but times it before the people had arrived. It does not seem unreasonable to suppose that the difference in the times is the key that harmonises the accounts. The question suggested by Jesus to Philip alone, and answered by him only, worked in the latter's mind all day; and, when the evening came on, his answer is again quoted by the disciples. John will then have fused into one the two conversations at the beginning and end of the day. The question was "to prove" Philip; that is, to see whether he had so grasped Christ's power as to answer, "We need not buy, for Thou canst supply." Does not Christ do with us thus still? He takes us, as it were, into His confidence, with interrogations that try us, whether we can rise above the level of visible resources, and believe in His unseen power.

Philip is always strong in his appreciation of what he can see. When Nathanael said to him, "Can any good thing come out of Nazareth?" all he had to say was, "Come and see,"—the best answer he could have made, but not the less characteristic. He broke in upon the sacred words in the upper room with, "Show us the Father." So here he sticks to the visible, and, running his eye over the crowd, makes a rough-and-ready calculation, the data of which we do not know, that some seven pounds might get a mouthful apiece for them. He was a man of figures, and believed in statistics, and, like some other folk of that sort, he left out one small factor in his calculation,—namely, Jesus Christ. When we have to deal with Christ's working—and when have we not?—the audacity of a faith that expects great things, though there is nothing visible on which to build, is wiser and more "practical" than the common sense that creeps along the low levels of "fact," and does not see the one all-important fact that we have a Divine Helper at our sides.

Then comes the exhibition of the poor resources of the disciples. Philip and Andrew were fellow-townsmen, and appear together (John i. 44 ; xii. 22). Note how the greater personality of Peter overshadows his brother, who is known to the readers rather by his relationship than for himself. Barley-loaves were the poor man's food, and one loaf per thousand was little. Two small fishes were still more ludicrously disproportionate to the case. The disciples' own stores seem to have been empty, and they would probably have been hungry though no crowd had come. Would Jesus have wrought a miracle to feed Himself? Christ's preparation for making our poor resources adequate is to drive home the consciousness of their insufficiency. When we have gone down into the depths of our own impotence, and seen that the work we have to do is far too great for our own strength, which is weakness, we are fit to receive His with rejoicing and overcoming might. We must be emptied of self if we are to be filled with God.

The next point is the seating of the hungry multitude. "Make the men sit down" was a test for both disciples and crowd. It would kindle wonder and expectation, and neither would have obeyed, unless some faint germ of faith, at least in His power to spread a table even there, had been quickened in them. At most, they anticipated food, and the measure of their expectation was the measure of His gift. A rudimentary trust brought corporeal blessings. It impelled to obedience, and obedience was rewarded according to its impulse and their need. John remembers still, after all these years, the flush of the spring grass on which the ranks of wondering, waiting people sat by the quiet lake. "Jesus therefore took the loaves." That is one of John's significant "therefores." If we sit down as He bids us, our mouths will not long be empty. If we do what He tells us to do, we shall get the food which we need. Our business is to obey and wait patiently in confidence; and His is to open His hand, when we are seated, and let the mercy drop on us. "Trust in the Lord, and do good; . . . verily thou shalt be fed."

Next comes the miracle itself. Two points only are noticed,—the thanksgiving and the distribution. According to the reading of the Revised Version, no mention is made of the disciples' agency as the almoners of Christ's gift, but His solitary figure fills the canvas. His tone or expression must have made that thanksgiving memorable, for, in verse 23, the place is referred to as "where they did eat bread after that the Lord had given thanks." The manner of the miracle and the point at which the multiplication occurred are left obscure. But that allusion in verse 23 seems to imply that it took effect at the moment of the prayer, which John calls "thanks" and the Synoptics "blessing."

What are the lessons of the "sign"? It teaches Christ's care for all forms of human want. It reveals His continuous working as Sustainer of physical life. In the miracle, some of the links ordinarily present in the chain which binds physical results to the Divine will were absent, but their absence or presence does not affect the reality of the connection between the staple from which it hangs and the last visible effect. The cause of all physical phenomena is the will of God, and that will works in and through Jesus Christ, in whom is life, and without whom nothing created subsists. He is Sustainer as well as Creator. He holds the stars in His hand, and He opens His hand, with the print of the nail in it, and satisfies the desires of every living thing.

But the great lesson of the miracle is that which our Lord Himself drew from it, in the following discourse on the bread of life, which we have to study in our next lesson, and may therefore leave for the present.

The result of the miracle is next presented in two ways,—the abundance left over, and the people's excitement. As to the former, note that the "broken pieces" are not the crumbs that littered the grass after the feast was over, but the pieces broken for distribution. John alone records that Christ commanded the gathering. He thereby taught economy in the use and storing of His gifts, and bade the disciples recognise that dependence on His miraculous power does not absolve from the exercise of ordinary prudence.

But if we regard the whole incident in that symbolic aspect in which He Himself presents it in the subsequent discourse, this abundant overplus and the care taken of it are fruitful of instruction. Men, women, and children, all found enough in the bread from His hands. The world scoffs at the barley-bread which Jesus gives, which seems coarse to palates spoiled by the world's confectionery; but it gives life to the eaters. If any man wants dainties that will tickle his diseased or fastidious appetite, he will have to go elsewhere for them; but if he wants bread, to stay his hunger, let him go to Jesus, who is "human nature's daily food."

But not only was there enough for each, but the twelve baskets were filled—one carried by each apostle, probably—with the food that had been prepared, and was not needed. "The gift doth stretch itself as 'tis received." Other goods and possessions perish with using, but this increases with use. The more one eats, the more there is for him to eat. All the world may live on it for ever, and there will be more at the end than at the beginning. In Christ's gift of the bread of life there is always a certain unappropriated overplus, a quality of infinity of resource, which surpasses our present power of reception, and encourages us to hope for larger possession when our faith is enlarged. That unrealised possible attainment is not to be left unheeded, but to be gathered up in the baskets of our growing faith, our more ardent desire and more lowly obedience, that it may be food for to-morrow, when we are able to make it our own. The unwon treasures of His grace should stimulate endless hope, aspiration, and effort. To-morrow shall be as this day, and much more abundant. That hope is folly, and worse, if cherished in regard to any life but a Christian life. Not to cherish it in regard to the Christian life is to fall beneath our privileges and to lose the unused abundance prepared for us by the Master of the feast.

The effect of the miracle on the crowd was simply to work them into an unwholesome fever of carnal Messianic hopes. How true to human nature their exclamation is! "A prophet that can give bread,—that is the sort of prophet for us. We can understand that kind of Messiah. The Samaritan heretic hoped for a Messiah who would teach all things. We do not care for teaching; give us loaves." Alas! the crowd has not got much further than this even now. They had much rather have some one who would find them bread without working for it, than one who would bring God's love and grace to them. Show them how to make money, or put them in the way of increased material comfort or prosperity, and they will hail you as a man of men, and build a monument to you when you die. But how many of us have no reverence for Jesus because we do not care for the gifts He has to bring!

LESSON VIII

True Work for True Bread

St. John vi. 26-40

26. "Jesus answered them and said, Verily, verily, I say unto you, Ye seek Me, not because ye saw the miracles, but because ye did eat of the loaves, and were filled.

27. Labour not for the meat which perisheth, but for that meat which endureth unto everlasting life, which the Son of man shall give unto you: for Him hath God the Father sealed.

28. Then said they unto Him, What shall we do, that we might work the works of God?

29. Jesus answered and said unto them, This is the work of God, that ye believe on Him whom He hath sent.

30. They said therefore unto Him, What sign showest Thou then, that we may see, and believe Thee? what dost Thou work?

31. Our fathers did eat manna in the desert; as it is written, He gave them bread from heaven to eat.

32. Then Jesus said unto them, Verily, verily, I say unto you, Moses gave you not that bread from heaven; but My Father giveth you the true bread from heaven.

33. For the bread of God is He which cometh down from heaven, and giveth life unto the world.

34. Then said they unto Him, Lord, evermore give us this bread.

35. And Jesus said unto them, I am the bread of life: he that cometh to Me shall never hunger; and he that believeth on Me shall never thirst.

36. But I said unto you, That ye also have seen Me, and believe not.

37. All that the Father giveth Me shall come to Me; and him that cometh to Me I will in no wise cast out.

38. For I came down from heaven, not to do Mine own will, but the will of Him that sent Me.

39. And this is the Father's will which hath sent Me, that of all which He hath given Me I should lose nothing, but should raise it up again at the last day.

40. And this is the will of Him that sent Me, that every one which seeth the Son, and believeth on Him, may have everlasting life, and I will raise him up at the last day."

IF we take into account the Jews' question to which the beginning of this lesson is an answer, we have in it four pairs of sayings by them, and replies by Jesus.

Theirs are three questions,—"When camest Thou hither?" "What must we do?" "What dost Thou work?"—and a petition, "Give us this bread." His words follow the channel marked by theirs, but yet have a progress of their own, and reach their climax in His full disclosure of Himself as the bread of life (ver. 35). There is then a slight pause in the discourse, and verses 37-40 have neither the metaphor of the bread nor any personal address, but are our Lord's declaration of the great purposes and certain issues of His work of lowly obedience to the Father's will, which issues should be reached, whether these men came to Him or no.

I. We have in verses 26 and 27 Christ's discernment of their low motives and disclosure of the only worthy aim of human effort. The Jews had spoken in their question as if they were surprised and had the right to be aggrieved that He had left them almost by stealth, and so given them the trouble of coming all the way back, across to Capernaum, to find Him. They mean to say, "Surely our eagerness to make Thee a king deserved at least more recognition than this." That surprised "when" really meant an offended "why."

Jesus, as ever, answers thoughts, not words. The surface of the question needed no answer; for the miracle had been wrought as evening came on, and now it was morning, and the passage of the lake must have been in the night. The question was inane and superfluous, and is treated as such; but the spirit which prompted it needs correction. So our Lord first cuts deep into the questioners' hearts, and lays bare the gross, sensuous nature of their admiration for and seeking after Him. They had seen the "sign," but it was no sign to them. All they saw or cared for was the loaves. This dissection of motives lays bare a truth concerning a wider circle than that which first heard it. The fatal predominance of earthly tastes and appetites, which dulls perception of and desire after higher good, besets us all. Religion itself is often recommended for the sake of its material advantages, and still more often neglected because we much prefer loaves to signs.

While verse 26 thus sets in clear light the often unconscious earthward gravitation of tastes and desires, verse 27 points to the one worthy aim of human effort, and in paradoxical form shows the means of attaining it. "The meat which perisheth" is, by its transiency, proved insufficient; and the life which is full of toil to win it, in any of its forms, sumptuous or coarse, dainties or bare necessaries, is shown to be too low-pitched. They labour for naught who labour for anything short of that which is permanent in its effects and nourishes eternal life. The description of this only sufficing possession as the "meat which abideth unto eternal life" is entirely parallel with that to the Samaritan woman, of the water springing up unto life eternal; and the whole course of the two dialogues is similar.

How different men's lives would be if they had clearly before them the only worthy aim! That being plain, how is it to be secured? Jesus answers by a double word, which sounds contradictory,—"work," "the Son of Man shall give." The solution of the paradox follows presently. Here it is enough to notice that, since it is a gift, the "work" does not earn it, and since there is to be work, it is not an arbitrary gift. The Giver of living water is the Giver of this bread. That claim, however lofty, is advanced in lowliness, and made to depend wholly on the Father's destination and designation of Him.

II. Verses 28 and 29 give the second turn in the conversation. The questioners do not resent rebuke, nor refuse obedience. It says something for them that their question goes straight to the important point of what they were to do. They are ready to do it, though they understand little about the bread spoken of by Him. But they take the "work," which He has been enjoining, in an entirely external sense, as is shown by that significant plural which they use. They had caught half of Christ's sentence, and the other had passed by them like idle wind. A heap of separate acts, such as God required, seemed to them what He meant; and now they want direction as to what these are. When some dim glimpses of what it is worth while to live for are caught, men immediately want to set about doing things to secure the aim. Such a state of mind is better than gross earthliness, but it is only twilight.

Christ's answer is divinely deep and simple. He sets one "work" against the mass of "works" which they thought would be needful. He declares that the single work which God requires as the condition of the gift is faith in the Son of Man, its Giver. To "believe on" is more than simply "to believe," with which lower act of the mind the Jews presently confound it. Here, then, is set forth in germ the whole truth as to the conditions of eternal life, and as to the relations of faith and works. Not a multitude of meritorious deeds, but the one act of trust; not the mere credence of His words, but the moral act of reliance on Him, is the way to receive His gift.

That faith is the seed of all the manifold "works of God" which a man can do; and they who have that faith will necessarily abound in these, and labour in all that they do to be well-pleasing to Him, and, even when toiling for perishable goods, will have an aim beyond these, and will labour for Him, and, whether they eat or drink, will do it in remembrance of the Giver of their eternal life.

III. Verses 30-33 give the next stage. The invitation to faith meets more opposition than the exhortation to work. So it always does. Twenty-four hours had not passed since they had seen the miracle which had wrought them to the pitch of wishing to make a king of Him, and now they are asking for a sign. Were their memories short? or was it not rather that they felt that something more was contained in His call for faith than they had thought of as in Him, and that they felt that the loftier claims demanded fuller attestation? The reference to Moses and the manna is relevant only if some vague idea was in their minds that Jesus was claiming to be at least another Moses, if not something more. But note how they degrade the idea of faith to that of simple credence, and how they make outward signs the only ground of the poor, starved thing they call "belief." Is there not, too, in their reiteration of Christ's own word in their question "What dost Thou work?" almost a scoff, as if they had said: "Work indeed! Time enough to tell us to work and to believe Thee, when Thou hast done something to warrant belief and to vindicate Thy right to command"? Evidently they are beginning to resist, and admiration and docility are passing into critical withdrawal.

Our Lord's answer is marked as solemn and important by the twofold "verily." He, first, with infinite majesty and calm, sets aside the suggested parallel with Moses, which doubly fails in that the latter was not the giver, and in that manna was not truly bread from heaven. Note the contrast between the past gift of the manna and the present (and continuous) gift of the bread. Note the claim of unique relationship between Him who has just called Himself the Giver, and the Father who in and through Him gives. Note the emphatic collocation of words in the original, "the bread out of heaven, the true." That bread is the reality of which all earthly food, even miraculous manna, is but the symbol. It, and only it, truly feeds men. The wondrous characteristics of that bread are then set forth in verse 33. It is the direct gift of God, it is "that which cometh down out of heaven" in continuous descent to hungry souls, it not only sustains but gives life, and it is meant for the whole world.

IV. No wonder that such words should stir desire for such a gift. The Samaritan woman's petition for the gift of the water to save her from thirst and toil is on the same level as this cry, "Evermore give us this bread." Deeply tainted with gross material misconceptions of some mysterious outward good, the people are yet touched with longings, and recognise His power to give what they need. That cry never goes to Him in vain, however dense the clouds of ignorance and error through which it rises to Him. Therefore the point is reached at which He can draw back the last veil, and show the truth in its brightness. Some eyes will be dazzled and turn away, but some may look and live.

At all events, the disclosure is the next step in answering the cry. Jesus gives the bread by declaring Himself to be the bread, and inviting us to Him that we may take it by faith. The full disclosure of Himself is again a parallel to that to the Samaritan woman. If we keep the immediately preceding description of the characteristics of the bread of God in view, how wonderful these words become! In them Jesus asserts His descent from the Father, His power to give life and to feed, with the only true nourishment, all the wants of every soul. Think of a man saying this to men, and, what is more wonderful still, getting men to believe him, and millions of them to answer, "Yes, we have tasted this bread, and know all that he said is true." He gave Himself to these Jews when He declared who He was, and invited them to come that they might hunger no more. He gives Himself to us, whom He invites to "believe on Him"; and He teaches us that coming is believing, and access to Him as possible for us as for those who stood by Him. If we exercise that faith which is coming to Him, we shall neither know the weakness of hunger nor the pangs of thirst; but will be strong with the nourishment of our powers, and glad with the satisfaction of our desires, as they only can be who eat the bread of life and drink the living water.

Verse 35 fully discloses the nature of the bread, the blessed results of possessing it, and the condition of receiving. But the sad fact that the listeners had not exercised that condition, as was obvious from their very petition, which proved them blind to the higher meanings of His sayings and to His true character, presses on His spirit, and draws out the lament and indictment which close His direct address. Verse 36 refers to a previous saying, probably that in verse 26, the inner meaning of which is truly preserved in the different form of this verse. The Jews had just asked for a sign, that they might see and believe. He tells them that they had seen Him, the greatest of signs, and that the sight had not led to belief. Sadness, wonder, and blame blend in that saying. That we should see Jesus, and not believe on Him, is the mystery and tragedy of the world, and is, alas ! repeated to-day.

V. Verses 37-40 are separated from the preceding in tone, by the absence of reference to the bread, and by the cessation of personal address. Probably a pause in Christ's utterance went before them. He seems to be staying Himself, in face of the people's unbelief, by gazing on the certain success of His work, quite as much as to be holding forth yet more attractively the blessed results of coming to Him, in still another attempt to win their faith. Both strains are blended in these wonderful words. Verses 37 and 38 sound principally the former, and verses 39 and 40 mainly the latter, but in neither case exclusively. "What if some did not believe?" Their unbelief shall not make the "purpose of God without effect." For "all that the Father giveth Me shall come to Me," where the neuter form is to be noted, as presenting the body of believers in all ages and lands as a definite whole, and the stress of the assurance is to be observed, as being shall "reach Me,"—not merely come towards, but attain to.

Then, in the next clause, the individual members of that whole are made prominent, and stress is laid on His welcome of each. Men come to Him, not in a mass, but one by one. Faith is intensely personal, and the wicket-gate lets in only one at a time. The blessed assurance of welcome is familiar to us all, but its remarkable connection is often passed by unnoticed. Here it is represented as the result of the perfect docility and submission of the Son to the will of the Father. The fact of a man's coming to Him by faith is the sign to Him that this man is the Father's gift to Him, and therefore He takes him to His heart. In all His earthly and heavenly work of redemption, whether it be His incarnation, life, death, reign in heaven, or reception and perfecting of believers, He is obedient to the Father, and does nothing of Himself. Therefore He was patient and undismayed, when men believed not. Therefore, too, we may go to Him, assured of a welcome.

Verses 39 and 40 present the glorious issues of faith in a double form, of which the similarities and the differences are equally noteworthy. "The will of Him that sent Me" in the true reading in verse 39 becomes in verse 40 "the will of My Father," so that the filial relationship is made emphatic and declared to be unique ("My Father"). In verse 39 the neuter form appears, and the objects of Christ's care are described as "that which He hath given Me"; the totality being the main thought, and the security of its present protection and certainty of its future life being considered as resting on the Father's gift and the Son's obedience; while in verse 40 the same persons are individualised, and described according to their own act of faith, which ensures His response of eternal life.

In verse 39 the present blessedness of believers is regarded as being safe keeping; in verse 40, as being everlasting life. But the two types merge in the final issue, though even there the one reads "it" and the other "him." The resurrection of the body is the necessary crown of that safe keeping and communicated life, which are the believer's privilege here. That glorious issue, without which the present experiences of the believer would be futile and the whole of his earthly life a confounding riddle, is wrought by Jesus Himself, as is emphatically claimed by the majestic "I" which the original underscores, so to speak, by its position, in the fortieth verse. He who feeds on the bread of life here cannot die. The resurrection to life must come as the copestone of redemption. Without it the building stands, would stand, a ruin, and the taunt would be justified, This Jesus began to build, and was not able to finish.

LESSON IX

"That Rock was Christ"

St. John vii. 31-44

31. "And many of the people believed on Him, and said, When Christ cometh, will He do more miracles than these which this man hath done?

32. The Pharisees heard that the people murmured such things concerning Him; and the Pharisees and the chief priests sent officers to take Him.

33. Then said Jesus unto them, Yet a little while am I with you, and then I go unto Him that sent Me.

34. Ye shall seek Me, and shall not find Me: and where I am, thither ye cannot come.

35. Then said the Jews among themselves, Whither will He go, that we shall not find Him? will He go unto the dispersed among the Gentiles, and teach the Gentiles?

36. What manner of saying is this that He said, Ye shall seek Me, and shall not find Me: and where I am, thither ye cannot come?

37. In the last day, that great day of the feast, Jesus stood and cried, saying, If any man thirst, let him come unto Me, and drink.

38. He that believeth on Me, as the Scripture hath said, out of his belly shall flow rivers of living water.

39. (But this spake He of the Spirit, which they that believe on Him should receive: for the Holy Ghost was not yet given; because that Jesus was not yet glorified.)

40. Many of the people therefore, when they heard this saying, said, Of a truth this is the Prophet.

41. Others said, This is the Christ. But some said, Shall Christ come out of Galilee?

42. Hath not the Scripture said, That Christ cometh of the seed of David, and out of the town of Bethlehem, where David was?

43. So there was a division among the people because of Him.

44. And some of them would have taken Him; but no man laid hands on Him."

THIS seventh chapter carries us into the midst of the glad stir in Jerusalem at the Feast of Tabernacles, and vividly reproduces the contending opinions and feelings about Jesus. There were three parties,—the "multitude," or the crowds of pilgrims, who were favourably disposed to Him, but wavering and easily swayed backwards and forwards as crowds are; the "Jews," the section who clung to carnal Messianic hopes, and could not but be against such a Messiah as Jesus; and the official class, divided into Pharisees and chief priests, the latter being mostly Sadducees, and violently antagonistic to the former, but one with them in hatred of Jesus. The chapter rings with the Babel of these discordant voices. Our lesson begins in the midst of the clamour, and may be considered with reference to the two sayings of our Lord which it contains.

I. We note then, first, His prophecy of departure, with its occasion and result (vers. 31-36). The calm boldness of our Lord's teaching in the temple, and the silence of the rulers, had impressed both the floating population of pilgrims and some of the residents in Jerusalem; but the latter had been alienated by His further declarations, while many of the former had been drawn to Him with a fuller faith thereby. Mark the "believed *on* Him" in verse 31, which expresses reliance, and not mere credence. This faith was real, though imperfect, as being founded on "signs." It was not bold enough nor perhaps certain enough to affirm, but only to whisper a question.

But those who have reached the point of asking what more the Christ could do than this man does, are not far from answering their own question with a full confession. The action of the rulers was precipitated by reports of these "murmurings"; for any spark might set the excited crowds in a blaze. It was humiliating for Jewish officials to have to stifle the national hope in which the Pharisees, at all events, shared; but that was the price they had to pay for place and power under Rome. The decision to arrest Jesus marked a new stage in the conflict of Divine love with unbelief, and John is careful to note its occasion in the people's ominous question, and its result in our Lord's saying.

That saying was apparently spoken in public, in the hearing of His would-be captors. If we try to realise the circumstances, the few calm words become majestic and pathetic. We note their recognition that this was the beginning of the end, a further stage in the struggle. The "little while" was but about six months, and this abortive attempt was like a signal-gun which opens a battle. But Christ's consciousness that the term of His continuance depends on Another than them is equally audible in the words. He knows that whatever the rulers may attempt, He will be with them still, and that when He leaves them, it will be His own act. His "hour" will tick out all its minutes before it strikes. He will not leave off nor be dragged from His work till it is done. The completion of His message is guaranteed to Himself and assured to men by the thought of "Him that sent" Him.

How eloquent of a unique relation to life and death and the future life is that calm word, "I go"—not I am driven; for men and death are impotent against Him, unless He wills to die—"to Him that sent Me" as a faithful messenger with an accomplished errand, returning to, not entering for the first time, the land beyond! It is no human consciousness merely that fronted the excited crowd and intending captors with such words. They open a glimpse into the Divine depths of His spirit.

But even in that hour of peril He thinks less of Himself than of men, and turns to these listeners with almost a wail of sad forecast, through which the tone of beseeching is heard. The incarnate Wisdom laments even while He foretells, as did the personified Wisdom in the Book of Proverbs, "They shall seek Me diligently, but they shall not find Me." The sad prophecy does not refer to penitence, but to the vain longings and futile seekings which have been that strange nation's bitter food ever since. The whole tragedy of its history is condensed into a sentence. Like all prophetic threatenings, it was said that it might not have to be experienced, and mercy shaped His lips to stern speech.

Why would their seeking be vain? Because they had not the conditions needful for that place and state of communion with the Father, whither He was going, and to which He only can lead any of us. Earthly-mindedness shuts us out from heaven and from finding Christ here. If we are to be with Him there, we must have sought Him here, with that true desire and seeking which ever finds. Mark that He "is," even when on earth, where He goes when He leaves earth. Mark, too, the tone of invitation to make the best use of the "little while." Conscious security till His work is done, prophetic warning and loving call to present faith, are all contained in these words.

The gross misunderstanding of them comes from the deafness of prejudice and hate, which left unnoticed the plain declaration "to Him that sent Me," in order to point a gibe at a Messiah who, when found out as an impostor at home, would carry His foolish "teaching" to the Gentiles. John is fond of recording sayings of enemies which the irony of Providence fulfilled. Like Caiaphas, these scoffers were wiser than they knew, and their taunt shadowed the actual course of the gospel. "Seeing ye condemn yourselves as unworthy of eternal life, lo, we turn to the Gentiles."

II. We have, secondly, the great call on the great day of the feast. The promise to the Samaritan woman is repeated and expanded in the temple-court. The well-known ceremonial of the water-drawing on the seven days of the feast naturally suggested it; and if, as seems probable, that rite was omitted on the last day, its very omission made Christ's words the more emphatic. They point, however, to the historical fact commemorated by the rite, and not only to the rite itself; namely, to the miracle in the desert, when the thirsty crowds saw the precious stream pouring from the rock. So here, again Jesus lays His hand on the great facts and thoughts of the old order, and claims to be that which they shadowed. This Gospel of John, which we are sometimes told is anti-Jewish, is really saturated with reminiscences of the earlier revelation; and in it Jesus claims to be the true temple, the reality of what the serpent typified, the real manna, the water-yielding rock, the pillar of cloud and fire, and the true Paschal Lamb.

The general idea contained in the emblem here needs no elucidation. Whatever thirst or longing desire is felt by man, Jesus will satisfy it. We stand awed as well as attracted by the majestic and unconditional universality of the promise. Who is this who fronts the whole race of men with open arms of invitation and calm confidence in His sufficiency for all the wants of every man? What majestic assurance in that "Me"! What wide-stretching, deep-reaching, individualising mercy of invitation in that "any man"! What universal invitation and Divine simplicity of conditions in that "let him come"! What wealth of promise that no coming can be vain, in that collocation "let him come . . . and drink"! Coming is believing; believing is sure to bring partaking; partaking is sure to still all painful desire. And all this blessedness is offered to every man down the ages and through the world; for every man thirsts, and may therefore come.

Nor does the gift stop with the satisfaction of the comer's own needs. He becomes a fountain for the slaking of others' thirst. Note Christ's own explanation of "coming," as synonymous with "believing on" Him. What "Scripture" is here quoted by our Lord? No Old Testament passage says in so many words, "Out of his belly shall flow," etc.; but there may be allusions to several, such as Isaiah lviii. 11. The difficulty of finding words analogous to those apparently quoted may be lightened if we refer to the original incident of the flowing stream from the rock in the wilderness; for there we read, "There shall come water out of it" (Exod. xvii. 6).

If this be recognised as the source of the quotation, we have the great thought that they who come to that Rock, and slake their own thirst there, become, in their measure of union with Him, as rocks yielding water for other thirsty souls. The result of real communion with Jesus Christ is not terminated in the rest, as of satisfied desires, which it brings, but passes on further to make us the medium of bringing like blessings to others. The end of personal religion is not personal reception, but communication, for which reception is the indispensable prior requisite. If a professing Christian has no impulse to impart, he had better examine himself whether he has drunk of the water of life. The paradox is true that we slake our own thirst by giving to others to drink. In England we have in some places what we call "swallow-holes," where a river plunges into the ground and is lost. Too many professing Christians are like those. But we are meant to be water-carriers, not water-drinkers only.

We have already seen, in the conversation with the woman of Samaria, that the water represents the gift of the Spirit; and that is the explanation which John gives in a parenthesis. He lays stress on the "shall" in verse 38, and regards it as pointing to a future gift. That thought is even more strongly expressed in the original, which might be read "were going to receive." Some modern critics, who know Christ's meaning better than John, think that he has made a mistake here, and that the "shall" in verse 37 is only the future of promise; but both the history of the Primitive Church and parallel sayings in this Gospel show that the evangelist's comment is right. The promise of satisfaction to individual thirst by coming to Jesus was for the then present as well as for every future; but that of the transformation of believers into fountains of spiritual influence was for the future only.

The change effected on the apostles at Pentecost is the best commentary on the words here. The same relation between the full gift of the Spirit and the glorifying of Jesus (mark the emphasis laid by the name on the humanity of our Lord) which is here indicated, is fully developed in our Lord's words in the upper room. The atoning work of Jesus had to be complete before the Spirit could dwell in men's hearts; and, since it is His office to apply to the soul that finished work, it evidently must be finished ere the Spirit could possess the material for His work. The "glorifying" of Jesus embraces not only His ascension, but His death. John takes the complementary view to Paul. To the latter, Christ's death is the lowest stage in His humiliation, while to the former it is the first step in His exaltation. Both thoughts are true. The zenith is the nadir. The cross is the throne. There the glory of endless pity, of Divine love, of Almighty power to redeem, shines forth.

The solemn calm of Christ's voice is followed by the recurrent jangle of conflicting tongues. The brief utterances in their direct form give a vivid impression of the eager controversies which surged round Jesus, like noisy waves on some steadfast rock. Two opinions were formed by those impressed by Christ's words, according to one of which He was "the Prophet" (Deut. xviii. 15), while others, who had got beyond the "murmurings" of verse 31, boldly acknowledged Him as the Christ. John details the objection to this view which came from some learned authorities, who knew their Old Testament in its letter, and demanded that Messiah should be born in Bethlehem. It did not matter what Divine wisdom, tenderness, purity, and power were in this Jesus. All these could not show Him to be Messiah. Where does He come from, not what He is, is the important point.

Better the ignorance that discerned His sweetness and bowed to His authority, than the learned blindness that pottered over the letter and let the spirit slip. Are there not a few Biblical scholars of that breed left yet? But John is struck again, much as when quoting the sarcasm in verse 35, with the thought that these wise people knew so little, and that the condition, the supposed non-fulfilment of which made their belief in this Christ impossible, whatever grace and truth He might disclose, had really been fulfilled, if they had only known it.

The same thing is continually recurring. Grave objections are made by partial knowledge, especially of the self-conceited and unspiritual sort, which fuller knowledge converts into arguments for the faith which they were supposed to destroy. Spiritual instincts are better guides to Jesus than microscopic literalism; and, if a man feels that he is thirsty, and is touched by Christ's gracious and majestic promise of living water, he need not pay much attention to objectors who would rob him of his faith because this or that bit of geography or history seems wrong. Probably it is right after all. Jesus was born in Bethlehem, though these cavillers thought that He was not, and knew that the Christ must be.

LESSON X

Freedom and Sonship

ST. JOHN viii. 31-47

31. "Then said Jesus to those Jews which believed on Him, If ye continue in My word, then are ye My disciples indeed;

32. And ye shall know the truth, and the truth shall make you free.

33. They answered Him, We be Abraham's seed, and were never in bondage to any man: how sayest Thou, Ye shall be made free?

34. Jesus answered them, Verily, verily, I say unto you, Whosoever committeth sin is the servant of sin.

35. And the servant abideth not in the house for ever: but the Son abideth ever.

36. If the Son therefore shall make you free, ye shall be free indeed.

37. I know that ye are Abraham's seed; but ye seek to kill Me, because My word hath no place in you.

38. I speak that which I have seen with My Father: and ye do that which ye have seen with your father.

39. They answered and said unto Him, Abraham is our father. Jesus saith unto them, If ye were Abraham's children, ye would do the works of Abraham.

40. But now ye seek to kill Me, a Man that hath told you the truth, which I have heard of God: this did not Abraham.

41. Ye do the deeds of your father. Then said they to Him, We be not born of fornication; we have one Father, even God.

42. Jesus said unto them, If God were your Father, ye would love Me: for I proceeded forth and came from God; neither came I of Myself, but He sent Me.

43. Why do ye not understand My speech? even because ye cannot hear My word.

44. Ye are of your father the devil, and the lusts of your father ye will do. He was a murderer from the beginning, and abode not in the truth, because there is no truth in him. When he speaketh a lie, he speaketh of his own: for he is a liar, and the father of it.

45. And because I tell you the truth, ye believe Me not.

46. Which of you convinceth Me of sin? And if I say the truth, why do ye not believe Me?

47. He that is of God heareth God's words: ye therefore hear them not, because ye are not of God."

THE remarkable description of the persons addressed in this conversation seems, at first sight, to blend incongruous characteristics, since John generally uses "Jews" to mean the section of the people who held fast by the hope of an earthly conqueror as Messiah, and were therefore opposed to Jesus. How could such persons "believe Him"? And how could believers be called "children of the devil," and charged with seeking to kill Jesus? The observation of the distinction between "believed on" (ver. 30) and "believed" gives the key. The former means reliance; the latter, mere credence. Such incomplete faith was quite consistent with retaining their carnal expectations, and must necessarily issue in falling away, when they understood Christ's true character. They had got to the point of believing Him the Messiah, but it must be their sort of Messiah. The words of our Lord, in verse 31, imply that these people were not yet "disciples indeed."

Our Lord's words in verses 31 and 32 are, then, His welcome and warning to very imperfect faith. He is willing to accept the least adequate recognition, and to deepen it. He lays down a condition, and gives a promise. The condition is "abiding in His word," where the singular is to be observed as marking His revelation as a whole, and the expression "abide in" as suggesting that "word" as the atmosphere in which the believer lives and moves. The converse representation of the word as abiding in us is also common in this Gospel. That word is the element in which we should live and the inward root of our lives. Faithful adherence to it develops rudimentary and half-seeing faith into completeness, as the triple promise holds forth.

True discipleship, in contrast to the crude adhesion given by these Jews; knowledge of the truth, which surpasses their present position both in respect to the sweep and elevation of that which is known and in regard to the manner of knowledge, which will be not mere head-work, but the fruit of experience and possession; and freedom brought about by that truth,—are the gifts waiting the disciple who abides in the Word. Intellectual freedom consists in the subjugation of the understanding to the truth which delivers from errors, prejudices, and the babble of human opinion. Moral freedom consists in the submission of the will to duty, which is the practical outcome of truth. To do as we ought is liberty; to do as we like is slavery. Spiritual freedom consists in the bowing down of the whole man to God, who is revealed by the truth, and to serve whom is to be master of self and things.

Skin-deep discipleship took offence at a promise in which it detected a view of its present condition which it resented. So it does to-day. Tell men that Jesus will redeem them from their sins, and they fire up at the implication that they are sinners.

How could these Jews assert that they had never been in bondage, with Egypt and Babylon in their history, and Roman eagles, visible from the temple, flaunting in "the castle"? They used the same strange power of ignoring disagreeable facts which blinds so many of us to our slavery. Sin's fetters are riveted when the bondsman lifts his manacled hands and protests his freedom. Pride of and trust in their descent, as if it gave them inalienable rights, and a vain assertion of liberty, were all that Christ's great promise evoked. The veneer of faith was very thin, and was already worn through and the baser core presented.

Our Lord takes up these two pleas in reverse order in His answer (vers. 34-38). First He sets forth the principles of true freedom; and, next, of true sonship. The solemn words in verse 34, introduced by that double "verily" which always indicates important and often unwelcome truth, and calls for special docility, tear away the flimsy veil, and disclose the fact which it is so easy and fatal to miss. True freedom or slavery is not an affair of political or social arrangements, but a condition of the spirit. The real bondage is that which enslaves the will and prevents doing right. The perverted state of the sinner, the terrible power of repeating itself which sin possesses, the impotence of the better nature to cast off the chains woven by acts, are all revealed as by a lightning flash in that awful saying, which shatters so much of our boasted independence, and is verified daily in the experience of those who cast off the restraints of virtue only to be tied and bound by the heavier fetters of vice. The stern brevity of the words adds to their force.

With like condensation, the fate of the slave is set forth in verse 35, and contrasted with that of the son. The boast of the Jews had been that, as sons of Abraham, they possessed inalienable freedom and secure tenure of their land. The answer lies in the difference between the permanency of slave and son, as the old story of Hagar and Ishmael showed it. The "slave" of verse 35 is necessarily the ideal of the class, and the reference to sin as the master is dropped. Slaves, whoever their lords, are not permanent dwellers; sons, whoever their fathers, are. This is true in relation to men and God. He who is sin's slave cannot claim the right of permanent enjoyment of God's blessings which he possesses for a time. Such secure continuance is the prerogative of a son. And the connecting thought implied is that slaves of sin cannot be sons of God.

The saying rang the knell of the national privileges of the Jews, and it discloses weighty and sad truths applicable to us; namely, the essentially transitory character of sinful men's possession of any outward blessings, and the dread sentence of exclusion, which must ultimately sever them from the family of God. There is something very terrible in these swift strokes as of a glittering sword, with which Jesus here so authoritatively shears through the outward shows, and lays bare realities and consequences.

As He passed from the specific idea of slave of sin to the general one of slave, so, with reverse motion, He next passes from the general idea of the sonship to the specific idea of "the Son"—of God, that is. Because the Son is ever in the Father's house, He can give true freedom. He does not yet say, "I am that Son," but He scarcely conceals that He is. What "the truth" does in verse 32 the Son does here, and, since that truth is equivalent to "My word," no doubt as to who this Son was could exist. He abides for ever in the Father's house, as He has told us all through the earlier lessons from this Gospel, being there even while incarnate. That abiding implies His full carrying out of the Father's will and wielding of the Father's power. Therefore He has power to break every yoke of bondage, and they who let Him show them their slavery and loose their chains are set free, and share in the prerogative of sons, and dwell for ever in the Father's house.

The second part of our Lord's answer deals, in the light of these truths, with the first part of the Jews' boast, and the remainder of the lesson turns on the true idea of fatherhood and sonship. The great truth is brought out, that true sons do the will and possess the likeness of their Father, and that thought is directed to shatter the two boasts of "the Jews" to be the children of Abraham and of God, and to force home to them their true descent.

In verses 37 and 38 Jesus admits their natural descent, and sets against it their attitude to Himself. Already they had passed from crude faith to hate, which will appear incredible only to those who do not know that no enemies are so embittered as disenchanted and renegade admirers. No doubt, Christ's charge drew into consciousness lurking feelings. Mark the reason He assigns for their hate, "My word hath not free course in you." Their beginning of belief did not grow. His truth, as more clearly unveiled, did not advance in them. Standing still is going back. If rudimentary faith does not mature, it rots. Our only safety is in the victorious progress of Christ's whole word in mind, heart, and life.

Verse 38 gives the reason for their non-acceptance of His word. He speaks what He has seen with His Father; they do what they have heard of theirs. Note the contrasts of "seen" and "heard," and of "with" and "from." Jesus claims superhuman vision of God and absolute correspondence of His revealing word with the Divine things beheld and revealed. Again, He "speaks"; they "do." For all His deeds are words in, and parts of, His word.

Thus far, our Lord keeps to the general thought of sonship as involving likeness, and does not plainly speak the names of the two fathers. We may by our actions make ourselves completely deaf to Christ's words; and nothing stops the ears of the spirit so surely as the wax of evil deeds consolidated into habits. Conduct betrays parentage.

Verses 39-41 reiterate the truth more sternly, in answer to the repeated boast of descent from Abraham. They differ from the preceding in saying plainly that there was absolute contradiction between the deeds of the patriarch and these, his descendants, in the designation of Jesus, in which His true manhood, His ministry of truth, and its source in God, are plainly declared, this being an advance on the previous clause, in which the Father was unnamed, and so preparing for the naming of the other "father."

In verse 41 the Jews show that they partly understood what Father Jesus claimed, and they follow Him on to His own ground, asserting that they too, because legitimately descended in the flesh from Abraham, are God's sons. The boast is shivered by the application of the same principle which shattered the former. But the principle is applied with a noticeable difference. Love to Jesus is "the spot of God's children." Think of one of us making men's love to himself the sign of being kindred with God!

How deep this saying cuts into the reasons for turning away from Jesus! Why will God's children necessarily love Jesus? Because He "came forth" in the past act of incarnation, which was His act, and "is come," standing there while He speaks, and "has not come," a phrase including past and present in one continuous whole, and the assertion regarding each being that He is "sent." So he that "loveth Him that begat loveth Him also that is begotten of Him."

Next, Jesus lays bare the ground of the Jews' failure in understanding as well as in love. "My speech" is less general and comprehensive than "My word." "Understand" is a subsequent process to "hear.' "Cannot" is a self-caused inability, the ground of which is immediately disclosed. Men can make themselves incapable of even hearing the word of Christ; and that general incapacity which comes from contrariety of moral disposition will prevent their grasping the meaning of His single utterances. A right judgment on His sayings requires spiritual susceptibility for His mission as a whole.

And now the awful revelation of the true paternity of these degenerate sons of Abraham is flashed forth. The inmost ground of want of love to Christ, and of incapacity to accept His word, is kindred with the great antagonist of God; and that kinship, it is to be observed, is distinctly declared as voluntary in the emphatic expression, "Ye *will* to do." Men are members of that family because they choose to be so, and do things contrary to God's will and accordant with Satan's "lusts." What are these lusts? Two are specified, both germane to the Jews' feelings to Jesus,—murderous hate and aversion to the truth.

The distinct reference to the Fall, by which death came on men, is to be noted; and there seems also a dim glimpse of a previous fall of the Tempter from "the truth." A spiritual being—man or angel—who has not "truth" within,—that is, no sincerity, uprightness of will, or affinity with the revelation of God, which is "the truth,"—cannot continue in it as his life's atmosphere. He has no lungs fitted to breathe it, and will suffocate there, like a man in water or a fish on land.

If we adopt the rendering of the difficult closing sentence of verse 44 in the Revised Version and in the Authorised Version, it carries on the allusion to the Fall and the Satanic lie then. "Of his own" points to the true diabolic nature, in contrast to that of the Son, who did and spoke nothing of Himself. Wherever such self-origination and casting off of filial obedience are, there are the "devil's marks," deep stamped. All his words are lies, his promises and his denials of God's threats. Himself a liar, he breeds lies in others. It is hard to believe that these solemn words of Christ's were only accommodated to Jewish superstition. They open a dread glimpse into the anarchic kingdom of antagonism to God, and press home the alternative,—either children of God or of the Devil.

The close of the lesson gathers all up to a point. So blinded were the Jews by the glamour cast by Satan's lies, that they rejected Jesus just because He spoke the truth. The highest truth has this for one of its credentials—that sinful men do not accept it. Tongues accustomed to the coarse pungency of leeks and garlic do not like manna. The devil's children naturally take to lies, and turn away from truth. Verse 46 in its first part gives as proof that He spoke the truth the unanswerable challenge to convict Him of sin. That glove lies in the lists still, and eighteen hundred years have produced no champion bold enough to lift it and say, "I will." Jesus asserts His sinlessness, and the world admits the claim. But does it accept the consequence, that sinlessness in action implies truth in speech? So He takes for granted here—and surely, if it be true that His manhood was utterly free from sin, the only explanation is to be found in the recognition of His sonship, and involved therein— the validity of His claim to be the perfect Revealer of the truth. On the basis of His flawless purity is solidly planted the searching question, "Why do ye not believe Me?" and no less solidly the final crushing unveiling of the ultimate reason for all unbelief, "Ye therefore hear them not, because ye are not of God."

LESSON XI

Jesus Seeing the Blind, and the Blind Seeing Jesus

St. John ix. 1-11, 35-38

1. "And as Jesus passed by, He saw a man which was blind from his birth.
2. And His disciples asked Him, saying, Master, who did sin, this man, or his parents, that he was born blind?
3. Jesus answered, Neither hath this man sinned, nor his parents: but that the works of God should be made manifest in him.
4. I must work the works of Him that sent Me, while it is day: the night cometh, when no man can work.
5. As long as I am in the world, I am the light of the world.
6. When He had thus spoken, He spat on the ground, and made clay of the spittle, and He anointed the eyes of the blind man with the clay.
7. And said unto him, Go, wash in the pool of Siloam, (which is by interpretation, Sent.) He went his way therefore, and washed, and came seeing.
8. The neighbours therefore, and they which before had seen him that he was blind, said, Is not this he that sat and begged?
9. Some said, This is he: others said, He is like him: but he said, I am he.
10. Therefore said they unto him, How were thine eyes opened?
11. He answered and said, A man that is called Jesus made clay, and anointed mine eyes, and said unto me, Go to the pool of Siloam, and wash: and I went and washed, and I received sight. . . .
35. Jesus heard that they had cast him out; and when He had found him, He said unto him, Dost thou believe on the Son of God?
36. He answered and said, Who is He, Lord, that I might believe on Him?
37. And Jesus said unto him, Thou hast both seen Him, and it is He that talketh with thee.
38. And he said, Lord, I believe. And he worshipped Him."

IT is remarkable that, while the other evangelists tell of miracles done at the request of others, all but one of those which John records were spontaneous on

Christ's part. That characteristic is strikingly brought out in this narrative. "He saw" the man. No one interceded for him. The disciples regarded him only as a theological problem. He himself sat silent, waiting for alms, all unconscious of the kind eyes fixed on him. But Jesus saw and pitied, recognised the will of the Father, and was about to intervene with healing when He was delayed by the question of the disciples.

Two ways of looking at suffering are suggested by the disciples' inquiry and Christ's answer. The former glanced at the blind man without pity. His was a common calamity, and interested them only as raising a doubt as to the persons to be blamed for it. Perhaps they remembered the saying to another sufferer, "Thou art made whole: sin no more." A commonplace of their religion was the connection between sin and suffering; and as, in this case, the affliction had been from birth, it strikes them as a curious question whether there had been sin in some previous state of existence, or whether it was a case of the children's expiating the parents' fault.

Christ's answer falls into three parts (vers. 3-5). First, He teaches the disciples and us how to look at suffering. So far as we are concerned, the chief consideration is that it gives opportunity for manifesting "the works of God" by helping to remedy it. No doubt there is a connection between sin and sorrow, and Jesus recognised it when He pronounced forgiveness to the palsied man before He healed his body. But to study misery as material for theological speculations or for censorious adjudging blame, is to miss its true purpose for us. Not what brought it, but what we can do to remove it, is the question for us. Speculations about "the origin of evil" may ossify the heart so that it throbs with no pity. That question is deeply interesting and important in its own place, but that place is not when we are standing beside the sufferer. Discuss the cause of the fire as much as you like, but try to put it out first and philosophise afterwards. The purpose of the evil around us, in reference to us, is to touch us with pity and summon us to help. "The works of God" are works of alleviation of affliction done by men who, in thus working, are carrying out the Divine purpose and imitating the Divine acts. We are likest God when we strive to reduce the sum of human misery.

Verse 4 unfolds the secret of Christ's unwearied diligence in His appointed task. The reading adopted in the Revised Version, "we must work," associates us with Him, and sets forth the great "must" which dominated His life as meant to dominate ours. But if that be the true reading, the difference between the Master and the servants remains; for our obligation is consequent on His mission, and His relation to the Father is that of being "sent" in a special manner. Jesus here shows us His inmost heart. That solemn "must" ruled all His life, and, in this Gospel, is often on His lips. But it was no unwelcome necessity reluctantly obeyed, but was inwoven with His deepest will and the occasion of His continual delight. Because His spirit said, "I delight to do Thy will," He was thereby "anointed with the oil of gladness above His fellows."

Jesus, too, as well as we, was stimulated to fill the moments with toil by the consciousness that the time was short. He, too, must make the most of the opportunities of earthly life; for, after it, the season for these gentle works of Omnipotence clothed in flesh would be ended. True, the "night" was really day, and the rest which followed earthly toil was to be filled with loftier work than giving this man sight; but still, the form of work which He then was doing could not be done in a near future. Therefore His course on earth, besides its grander and more recondite features, is marked by the homely virtue of hard work, and utilising every moment.

These two characteristics are to be reproduced by us, whether this verse is to be read "we" or "I." The quick response of a shoot of pity and love when we see sorrow; the consciousness of a great necessity, which we rejoice to obey, bidding us help the sufferers, and so do God's works; the unhasting, unresting diligence which marks the evening shadows lengthening, while so much of the harvest is unreaped, and therefore is a miser of time and prodigal of strength,—these are the signs of a true disciple. Let us leave the question of the cause of the misery to censorious and curious people, except so far as the knowledge of the cause may direct wise effort to cure; and let us feel that every sorrow which we see has a message and purpose for us, and is God's call to us to soothe and, if possible, remove it.

Verse 5 is the majestic utterance of His conscious power, which power here is present to His mind, as, if we may so say, the measure of His responsibility. He knows that He is "the Light of the world," and can give the lower light for the eyes, and the higher for the spirit, to this man, as to every man. Therefore He pauses before him, full of pity, of filial obedience, and of consciousness of power. The words are to be taken in their widest and deepest meaning, as declaring what John said in the prologue to the Gospel, that He is the Light of men, in all senses of that word, and to all. He did not cease to be "in the world" when He ascended, any more than He began to be in it when He was born; but the period of His earthly life had special modes of manifesting Him as the Light, and one of these was such a miracle as this. While, then, in one aspect, the saying is parallel to the preceding, in another it stretches far beyond it, and declares a presence and an influence coeval with creation and coextensive with humanity. Christ is the Light of the world in a sense in which none others are; but the same condescension which underlies the possible "we" preceding, associates us with Him in the name, and, derived though our radiance be, He calls His servants "the lights of the world." The name should be to us what here it was to Him, a call to let the light shine on darkened eyes.

The miracle proper is the smallest part of this narrative, and is distinguished by the special feature of our Lord's use of means, which was rare with Him, and in each case probably to be accounted for by the spiritual needs of the subjects. It might be a help to feeble faith, to a man who has not seen His gentle face nor marked the pity in His eye. The touch of His hand on the poor sightless eyes, and the clay laid there by it, would aid apprehension, and be a crutch for faith.

Another peculiarity is the healing at a distance, of which we have another example in the fourth chapter. The significance of the name "Siloam" was the reason for its place in the cure. The name refers either to the gushing out of the waters discharged from an underground channel, or, less probably, to their being a gift sent from God. Already in John vii. 37 the water from that spring was taken by our Lord as a type of Himself; and here the emphasis is to be laid, not on the fact that the blind man was "sent" to the fountain, but that He who was "sent from God" was the true agent in his cure.

Again, the method of cure suspends healing on obedience, as in the other case where the command "Stretch forth thy hand" was addressed to a man who could not stretch it out, but who, trying, became able. Compliance with Christ's conditions brings healing. For us the condition is faith. We have to wash in the true Fountain, "sent of God" for sin and uncleanness; and, if we do, we shall come seeing, and clean.

The buzz of talk among the neighbours is vividly given, and attests the conspicuous notoriety of the miracle. The blind man's character is strongly marked throughout. He sturdily adheres to facts, will not be tempted one inch beyond them, declines to speculate, or to profess to know anything more than he does know; has a touch of dry sarcasm and quick-wittedness, and, withal, docility very touching when combined with such independence. Therefore he gets the better sight, as told in the closing verses of the lesson.

His conceptions of Jesus had been steadily rising, from "the man Jesus" to "a prophet," and "from God." Opposition and the floundering of the Pharisees in trying to explain away his cure had led him to progressive preparedness for the fuller revelation. The excommunication left him sad, but unshaken. Jesus went to look for the outcast, as He ever does. The question "Dost thou believe?" is really an invitation to believe; and it is to be observed that our Lord here asks for faith in its deepest sense—namely, that believing on Him which we have had frequent occasion to distinguish from simply believing Him. It is reliance absolute and firm which He seeks. And the object of that faith is "the Son of God," in the full meaning of that great name, the whole significance of which yet waited to be revealed. How the strong, sturdy man who had held his own with the Sanhedrim, and given back sarcasm for threat, melts and bows in docility before Him whom he had such good cause to trust, and whose greatness had been slowly shining in on his newly seeing soul!

It is not blind submission which professes its readiness to accept further teaching from a teacher who has done so much for him. If Jesus were the prophet which His acts convinced the man that He was, then His words were to be taken as truth, whatever they declared or demanded. The recognition of Him as "from God," honestly followed out, will lead to something more wonderful still. Where there has been true adherence to present measures of light, and willingness to follow that light wherever it leads, Jesus will come and disclose Himself. Many a man has found that to be cast out by men is to be found by Christ, and that, when hunted from the fellowship of formalists, his solitude has been illumined by the sunshine of that face.

The answer of our Lord to the man's eager question is very beautiful. He does not say "I am He," but describes Himself by two characteristics, the first of which ("thou hast seen Him") touches delicately the obligation under which the man lay to Him, and the proof in the miracle of His love and power. "That thou canst see at all is My gift, and My better gift is that thou dost see Me." The second emphasises the wonderful fact that the Son of God stands in human form before him, and talks in familiar friendship. It is like the word to the Samaritan woman, "I that speak unto thee am He"; and both lay on our hearts the gracious and astounding mystery of incarnate love, by which the Son of God dwells among us, and men can speak face to face with Him as a man speaketh with his friend.

Thus flooded with light, the soul of this poor blind man bows in lowly adoration, compact of gratitude, awe, and loving trust, and worships the Bringer of sight to his eyeballs and of the better vision to his spirit. If we will listen to Jesus, He will talk with us; and if we will obey His conditions and go to the fountain "Sent," which is Himself, and wash there, we too shall see, and have for ours the irrefragable argument of experience with which this blind beggar pulverised the cavils of the Sanhedrim: "Whether He be a sinner or no, I know not: one thing I know, that, whereas I was blind, now I see."

LESSON XII

The Shepherd of Men

St. John x. 1-16

1. "Verily, verily, I say unto you, He that entereth not by the door into the sheepfold, but climbeth up some other way, the same is a thief and a robber.

2. But he that entereth in by the door is the shepherd of the sheep.

3. To him the porter openeth; and the sheep hear his voice: and he calleth his own sheep by name, and leadeth them out.

4. And when he putteth forth his own sheep, he goeth before them, and the sheep follow him: for they know his voice.

5. And a stranger will they not follow, but will flee from him: for they know not the voice of strangers.

6. This parable spake Jesus unto them: but they understood not what things they were which He spake unto them.

7. Then said Jesus unto them again, Verily, verily, I say unto you, I am the Door of the sheep.

8. All that ever came before Me are thieves and robbers: but the sheep did not hear them.

9. I am the Door: by Me if any man enter in, he shall be saved, and shall go in and out, and find pasture.

10. The thief cometh not, but for to steal, and to kill, and to destroy: I am come that they might have life, and that they might have it more abundantly.

11. I am the Good Shepherd: the good shepherd giveth his life for the sheep.

12. But he that is an hireling, and not the shepherd, whose own the sheep are not, seeth the wolf coming, and leaveth the sheep, and fleeth: and the wolf catcheth them, and scattereth the sheep.

13. The hireling fleeth, because he is an hireling, and careth not for the sheep.

14. I am the Good Shepherd, and know My sheep, and am known of Mine.

15. As the Father knoweth Me, even so know I the Father: and I lay down My life for the sheep.

16. And other sheep I have, which are not of this fold: them also I must bring, and they shall hear My voice; and there shall be one fold, and one Shepherd."

THE Pharisees' treatment of the blind man showed what tender shepherds they were, and their indignant "Are we blind?" betrayed their irritable self-conceit. Therefore Christ assails their consciences in this lesson, which must be taken in close connection with what goes before. We have, first, a picture of a true shepherd, and then the expansion and application of its two principal ideas.

I. The "parable" (vers. 1-5) sets forth the ideal of a true shepherd; but, since that ideal is fulfilled in Jesus, it is also His own portrait of Himself, though the personal reference is quite in the background. The picture is meant to rouse the consciences of the unworthy shepherds by showing them what they should be; but that application is also in the background. It is not always wise to say, "Thou art the man." It is often better to hold up the portrait of what a man should be, and leave him to say whether it is a likeness of him.

A true shepherd enters the fold by the door. A fold is an external organisation: in its original meaning here, the Jewish theocracy; for us, the Christian Church. This Gospel has all along been insisting on the activity of the eternal Word before incarnation; and therefore we must take it that from the beginning all true shepherds and guides—lawgivers, prophets, kings—entered on their office through Him. Honest men go in by the door. If we see one getting over the fence, we conclude that he is on no good errand. The unworthy teachers of that day had selfish ends to further, and, whether by stealth like "a thief" or by violence like a "robber," sought their own gain. They are dead and gone, but the warning is much needed by Christian teachers of all degrees. He is no true shepherd who does not derive his office from Jesus, and use it for Him. "Not ourselves, but Christ Jesus the Lord; and ourselves your servants," should be our motto. Reliance on one's own powers, entrance on such sacred tasks from one's own self-will, discharge of them for one's own advantage, either as regards money or glory, making anything but Jesus one's theme, are signs of being thieves, not shepherds. These are the dangers besetting all religious teaching. Conceit climbs high; the door is low-pitched, and a man must stoop to go in.

"To him the porter openeth." The meaning of this second trait is obscure. To treat it as mere embellishment seems scarcely reverent; to explain it as referring to recognition by ecclesiastical authorities is incongruous —for these are "shepherds." The explanation which sees in it the work of the Divine Spirit furthering Christ-derived and Christ-devoted work seems worthiest. He who enters on his service through the door will find a mighty power clearing away obstacles and prospering his goings.

Next we see the shepherd in the fold (ver. 3). His only weapon is his voice, and "the sheep" hear it. The presence in the fold of unworthy members is probably lightly indicated; but the main point is that prepared hearts recognise the truth, and in like manner the selective work of the shepherd may be glanced at, as well as the tenderness of the bond between him and the flock in that sweet phrase, "his *own* sheep." Each true Christian teacher will find some who will specially respond to his manner of setting forth the truth.

Diversities of gifts correspond to diversities of needs. Individualising care and tender knowledge of each are marks of the true shepherd. To call by name implies this and more. To a stranger all sheep are alike; the shepherd knows them apart. It is a beautiful picture of loving intimacy, lowliness, care, and confidence, and one which every teacher should ponder. Contrast with it the Pharisees' treatment of the blind man.

Having gathered his own sheep, the shepherd "leadeth them out." So we have next the shepherd and flock outside the fold. They are taken out to pasture and exercise, which, in the most wide application, suggests that the activities of life are to be regulated by the truth that religious teaching finds its goal in obedient conduct; that to do, and not to meditate or rest, is the end of man. But there is, probably, also a hint that the time for the separation between sheep and goats in Israel was at hand, and that Jesus was soon to call His own from the mass, and guide them to new pastures. The hint of the establishment of the Church apart from the synagogue is here.

But the main point in the sweet picture is the relation of confidence and close companionship between shepherd and sheep,—he going before; they, drawn by his voice, following, safe in his presence and secure from wandering, when behind him. Lessons for all Christian teachers lie on the surface; that is the ideal for them. They miserably fail if they are not leaders in holy living, just as disciples fail if they merely admire their voices, and do not follow their footsteps. Of course, through this ideal picture of what every true shepherd should be shines the actual realisation of it in Christ, who is Himself the

Shepherd whom He drew; but that is in the background.

II. The expansion and application to Christ of the figure of the door. Note that new phase of the idea, conveyed in calling it "the door of the sheep," not merely, as before, for the shepherds to go in by. Observe, too, the pause before developing the meaning of the emblem, to denounce again the "thieves and robbers." Here these must be false mediums of access to whatever the door leads to; that is to say, pretenders to open the way to God, to safety, and pasture. The omission of "ever" in the Revised Version and the present tense "are" show that the pretenders spoken of are cotemporaries of Jesus, though "before Him" as already exercising their false authority. In fact, He means the existing rulers, whose pretensions to give access to God are as baseless and inspired by the same self-seeking as their claims to be the true shepherds.

But that is but a momentary flash of lightning. He returns to set forth the wonders to which He admits, in words which only familiarity robs of their sublime self-consciousness. The picture has somewhat shifted. The flock are now outside, and the fold is not so definitely an organisation. It is rather the true home of wandering souls, the fold of God. Jesus here stands before the whole world, and, with universal invitation, witnessing to His claim of Divine universality of power, presents Himself as the medium by which every man may have all that he needs.

Three things are requisite for vigorous life,—security, a field for exercise of activity, and food. Jesus says that He will supply them all. The condition is entrance through Him, which is plainly tantamount to faith in Him as our sole means of access to God. Then comes security; for the figure of the flock is kept up, and "saved" has probably not so much the full Christian meaning as the general one of safety,—from outward disasters, which will not hurt us if we are in Him; from inward evil, which will not tempt if we dwell in the fold; and thus, finally, from everything outward or inward which could sadden, hurt, or stain our souls. The many temporary and partial deliverances are crowned by the final complete salvation. If we keep behind the breakwater, and cast anchor with Jesus between us and the wind, we shall ride out the storms. We shall, further, have the free exercise of powers. "Go in and out" means free, unrestricted activity. Both the contemplative and active sides of life are included. Within the fold is repose; without is healthful exercise. We must go deep into God if we would be blessed, and Jesus leads us into the secret place of the Most High, where we can renew strength and regain calmness. We must go out into the world; and Jesus gives us a pattern for action, motives for service, and new powers, as none else can. Christians should be complete men. But we must "go in" first, if we are to "go out" charged with blessing for others.

Further, Jesus gives provision for all true wants, food for all powers, desires, and aspirations, and He makes the desert yield supplies. Without Him, the world is like the burnt-up pastures after drought, where starving sheep mumble some dry stalks that crumble to dust in their mouths; but, with Him, it is like the same pastures after rain,—green with juicy grass.

The transition to the image of the shepherd is prepared for in verse 10, in which the persons ("thief," "I") are contrasted, the general truth applicable to a class ("cometh") set by the side of the single past coming which has abiding presence as result ("am come"), and the effects of the selfish teacher's lessons—which are robbing the true Owner of His sheep by making them partisans of a man, spiritual death and the destruction of what would nourish life—are presented in contrast with the life in its deepest and widest sense which He gives, and the abundance of all that will nourish and increase it.

III. We have the image of the shepherd applied to Jesus (vers. 11-16). "Good" means "beautiful" as well as "excellent," and suggests the gracious and lovely attractiveness of our Lord's character as Shepherd. Note the strangeness of a man's saying anything like this about himself. Is not Jesus harder to understand if we reject His Divinity than if we accept it?

But what is the one token that He is the Good Shepherd? His laying down His life. Here is a prophecy of His death, a claim that He lays down His life voluntarily as one might put aside a garment, a declaration that His death is "for the sheep," and the plain implication that it is the very centre and heart of His work, establishing His claim to be our Shepherd. True, the whole meaning and power of it are not revealed, but it is set forth as the climax of self-sacrificing care, and as the way of saving the flock from the wolf. We shall not understand Jesus, nor see the fairest beauty in Him, till we learn that His voluntary death for us is the keystone of His work.

The contrast now is with hirelings, not thieves. The wolf does what the thieves did,—kills and destroys. Whoever fills any office involving the care and guidance of men, and is swayed by mercenary considerations, will have a quick eye to see danger far off, and will look after himself, deserting duty to keep life. There are whole packs of wolves snuffing round every fold, and hirelings always have been, and will be, cowards. "Faithful unto death" he only will be who has caught his inspiration from Jesus, and does his work "all for love, and nothing for reward."

Another mark of the Good Shepherd is the perfect knowledge and sympathy between Him and the flock. "I know Mine own, and Mine own know Me." That throws a bridge across the gulf between us, and likens the humble upward movement of the dependent love, which is knowledge and possession, to the downward flow of that love which is Divine. His knowledge of us guarantees our safety and peace. "The Lord knoweth them that are His" is the seal stamped on the foundation, by which it "standeth sure." Ours of Him clings and trusts and grows, and is enriched by experience. But yet, with all differences, the lower is like the higher and the same sympathy and love look out of the eyes of the Shepherd and of the flock. Deep words, which we can only bow before in adoration, declare that the union of knowledge and love between Christ and us has its original in that ineffable union between the Father and the Son. The unknown is made to explain the known; and it does so if it helps us to feel how sacred, deep, and, in its possibilities, inexhaustible, is the bond which knits the humblest soul that follows the

Shepherd to Him whom he feebly loves and dimly knows.

These mysteries of intimacy will not seem impossible if we turn again to gaze on the blessed fact which founds them, even the death of Christ for the sheep. That sacrifice is the indispensable prerequisite if we are ever to come to this satisfying and wonderful communion of heart and mind with Him. Here Jesus declares that He will do what He has just said that a good shepherd must be ready to do.

And, as He sees the cross rising before His prophetic eye, the narrow bounds of the "fold" which then was melt away, and He sees the "other sheep" flocking to His call. The thought of the universality of His redemption is very frequently associated with His prevision of the cross, as if, before He suffered, He saw of the travail of His soul, and was satisfied. These triumphant words teach us the spirit in which we should look on the outlying regions as belonging to Christ, as containing some who are His, and as sure to be won for Him. They teach us the Divine necessity which lay on His Spirit, and should press on ours. They assure us that He is now fulfilling that "must," and will help His servants to fulfil it. They bid us lift our eyes beyond the narrow bounds of existing organised Christianity, and rouse our faith and expectations to embrace what He saw then. They set the final state of His Church before us. He shows us a "flock," not a "fold"; one, not because of a surrounding wall, but because of a central Lord and Leader. If the shepherd be in the midst, the sheep will couch round him, and be one because all are knit to the one Shepherd.

LESSON XIII

The Crowning Miracle

St. John xi. 21-44

21. "Then said Martha unto Jesus, Lord, if Thou hadst been here, my brother had not died.

22. But I know, that even now, whatsoever Thou wilt ask of God, God will give it Thee.

23. Jesus saith unto her, Thy brother shall rise again.

24. Martha said unto Him, I know that he shall rise again in the resurrection at the last day.

25. Jesus said unto her, I am the resurrection, and the life: he that believeth in Me, though he were dead, yet shall he live:

26. And whosoever liveth and believeth in Me shall never die. Believest thou this?

27. She saith unto Him, Yea, Lord: I believe that Thou art the Christ, the Son of God, which should come into the world.

28. And when she had so said, she went her way, and called Mary her sister secretly, saying, The Master is come, and calleth for thee.

29. As soon as she heard that, she arose quickly, and came unto Him.

30. Now Jesus was not yet come into the town, but was in that place where Martha met Him.

31. The Jews then which were with her in the house, and comforted her, when they saw Mary, that she rose up hastily and went out, followed her, saying, She goeth unto the grave to weep there.

32. Then when Mary was come where Jesus was, and saw Him, she fell down at His feet, saying unto Him, Lord, if Thou hadst been here, my brother had not died.

33. When Jesus therefore saw her weeping, and the Jews also weeping which came with her, He groaned in the spirit, and was troubled,

34. And said, Where have ye laid him? They said unto Him, Lord, come and see.

35. Jesus wept.

36. Then said the Jews, Behold how He loved him!

37. And some of them said, Could not this man, which opened the eyes of the blind, have caused that even this man should not have died?

Less. XIII.] The Crowning Miracle

38. Jesus therefore again groaning in Himself cometh to the grave. It was a cave, and a stone lay upon it.

39. Jesus said, Take ye away the stone. Martha, the sister of him that was dead, saith unto Him, Lord, by this time he stinketh: for he hath been dead four days.

40. Jesus saith unto her, Said I not unto thee, that if thou wouldest believe, thou shouldest see the glory of God?

41. Then they took away the stone from the place where the dead was laid. And Jesus lifted up His eyes, and said, Father, I thank Thee that Thou hast heard Me.

42. And I knew that Thou hearest Me always: but because of the people which stand by I said it, that they may believe that Thou hast sent Me.

43. And when He thus had spoken, He cried with a loud voice, Lazarus, come forth.

44. And he that was dead came forth, bound hand and foot with graveclothes: and his face was bound about with a napkin. Jesus saith unto them, Loose him, and let him go."

JOHN records seven miracles before the crucifixion, all deeply significant. The raising of Lazarus is the last, and, if we can compare miracles, the greatest. It crowns the whole, not only by its revelation of the Lifegiver, but by its disclosing of Christ's human sympathy and individualising love, the majesty of the manner of His work, the pathos and rich store of consolation for bleeding hearts hived in the inimitable narrative. The direct effect of the miracle in precipitating Christ's death is also part of the reason for the minute account of it. The story is as inexhaustible as inimitable, and we can only skim its surface. The material naturally gathers into four portions.

I. Jesus and Martha; the drawing forth of faith.—
It was like Martha to be in the way to get the news of Christ's arrival, and to rush to Him without telling Mary. Grief that can work is easier to bear than grief that sits still and broods. "If Thou hadst been here" is not meant for reproach, but regret, mingled with trust that somehow Jesus could have hindered the blow.

Sorrowful hearts are but too apt, like the man with the legion, to cut themselves with this sharp knife. We all know the bitter thought, "How different everything would have been, if only —— " Regret passed quickly into a wild hope, which did not venture to name itself. She means "resurrection" when she only dares to say "whatever." Perhaps she knew of the raisings of Jairus' daughter and the widow's son. But the wistful belief that Jesus could was shaded by a doubt if He would, and her words are a petition. The imperfection of her conception is obvious as regards Christ's relation to God and to His own gifts; but the strength of the faith, born of sorrow and sore need, is beautiful. Despair grasps Jesus, and is transformed into faith that dares to expect even impossibilities. Thick smoke-wreaths flare up, when they are once set on fire.

The purpose of Christ's treatment of Martha was to evoke and enlighten her faith, which, though not needful for the miracle, was needful for her getting the full good of it. So His first reply is intentionally indefinite. If the hope she expressed were deep and solid, she would apply the promise to the moment; if not, it would sound remote. Jesus grants requests, but often in such a form that faith is needed to perceive the grant. "The gift doth stretch itself as 'tis received." Will Martha take what is given, or spill the most of it by tremulous faith? Her answer is almost impatient, as it puts away the far-off prospect as all insufficient for present comfort. Heart's agony makes short work of religious commonplaces. It is a dreary, long road to "the last day," and she wants Lazarus now. How true to nature that putting away of the very hope that she had been cherishing! So swiftly does the mood change, and what seemed solid melt into cloud.

But this at least has been gained, that the thought of resurrection has been twice spoken, and the way prepared for the full glorious declaration which Jesus offers to her faith: "I am the resurrection." That sets right her notion of His relation to His gift, and, in its assumption of the power of His personality, contrasts with "God will give it thee." It also meets the sad postponement to a far-off future, and teaches that in Him standing by her side was power to effect a resurrection now as well as then. Whenever and however it takes place, it is His work.

The order of words is profoundly significant; for "resurrection" comes first, not simply as the subject in hand, but as being the issue of what is named second, "life." Jesus is the former because He is the latter, and partaking in resurrection is the certain issue of partaking in life. Therefore two paradoxes for sense are true on condition of union with Jesus by faith. If He is the resurrection, they who believe live, though they die. If He is the life, they who, in this mortal being, are united to Him by faith, never really die; for the name of death is not to be given to the physical fact, which does not touch the life eternal. United to Jesus, we are vital with a life over which the shadow called Death has no dominion; and having passed through the dark sea, as some bright stream may through a sullen lake, without losing its current or a drop of its waters, shall flow on beyond to meet the sunny ocean. The resurrection of all believers is the consequence of their possession of Christ's life.

These were stupendous truths to flash upon tear-dimmed eyes, and to be followed by the searching question, "Believest thou this?" But great truths are quickly assimilated by deeply moved souls, and lasting faith sometimes grows, or becomes conscious of its growth, as fast as Jonah's gourd. Martha's answer fully accepts the wonderful words, and is not rash credulity; for she builds her swift belief on rock when she says, "I *have* believed that Thou art the Christ." That faith had been slow to grow, but it prepared for the unhesitating acceptance of all that He showed her.

II. Jesus and Mary; sympathy with grief.—The work on Martha was done when her faith thus triumphantly closed with the great promise, and now she sought her sister. Apparently Jesus bade her go; for her words to Mary are scarcely her own inference. Her calling "secretly" indicates the natural wish to get rid of heartless "comforters," but the effort was vain. Mary's characteristic swift setting out did not shake off the conventional sympathisers, who understood sorrow so little that they would not let it have a moment of solitude to break down in, and be relieved.

Note the delicate difference between the sisters, in that while both say the same thing, and thereby show how monotonously they had said it to one another in the four dreary days, Mary falls at Christ's feet, and has no word of hope for "even now." The difference of character makes their treatment different. Martha got teaching; Mary, sympathy. Christ's tears would do more for her than words.

That picture of the emotion of Jesus is too sacred for cool comment. But we may reverently mark the token of Christ's true manhood, in that the sight of tears brings His, as well as in that He has tears to be brought. Surely, of all the signs of His manhood none is more precious than this. It sanctions sorrow, and sets its limits. It reveals the reality of His sympathy, the depth of His personal affection. It lets us see dimly that He could not take away grief without feeling its pressure, and that His work was not done without painful cost.

But tears were not all that the sight of sorrow evoked. That other phase of emotion, described in the margin of the Revised Version as "moved with indignation in the spirit," opens a glimpse into a deep region. What was the cause of this strange storm of anger which swept across that calm spirit? Surely the most worthy answer is that He saw in this one death and these two weeping sisters, as it were, one drop in the ocean of woes which covered the earth. He summons all the miseries of man before Him, and sees them all in connection with their cause, sin, and possibly the personal tempter, whose handiwork of murdering was so near. But that brief agitation did not delay His work; and the very fact that He felt it, even when the end of the sorrow was so near, shows how keen His sympathy was, and is, with transitory ills. If Jesus did not feel with us the pains which He knows are brief, what pains would He feel?

Another apparent taking of human conditions is His question—the only one of the kind in the Gospels—as to the situation of the tomb. But perhaps it was rather meant as an invitation to the "Jews" to do what they ask Him to do,—"come and see." An evident desire for publicity marks Him at this stage, and, knowing what would come of it, He courts the presence of witnesses. How natural the fresh burst of tears as they drew near the tomb! And how cool the criticisms of the curious group, some struck by the tokens of His affection, but not sharing it, and others half scoffing, and suggesting that His letting so dear a friend die discredited His power to cure a blind stranger! Malice is ingenious and shallow. Think of men having actually seen Jesus weeping, and having nothing else to say about it than this!

III. Jesus at the tomb.—Majestic calm of conscious, unbroken communion! The emotion is past, and the habitual calm majesty reassumed. The command to take away the stone is in accord with Christ's continual economy in the use of miraculous power. Whatever man can do is to be done by man; and, besides, the men whose hands rolled away the stone were made witnesses of the resurrection.

John has a delicate touch in reminding us of Martha's relationship to "him that was dead," as explaining the natural shrinking of her love from the exposure of the dear form in its dishonour. But she was faltering in her faith, or she would not have so spoken. Therefore Jesus puts out a hand to hold her up, as He did to Peter sinking, and His reminder of the previous conversation puts its true purport into other words. He had, in effect, told her that, if she believed, she would see the glory of God, when He had sought to draw out her faith, and spread before her astonished eyes the resurrection and the life which come by faith. Her faith was not the condition of the miracle, but it was of her enjoying (seeing) all that the miracle meant and prophesied. The outward fact might be seen by eyes all blind to the glory that shone in it.

With like majesty sounds the solemn thanksgiving before the mighty act. It was not a prayer, such as Martha had meant. He does not ask for a gift, but He gives thanks. He traces, indeed, as always, the miracle to the Father; for He does nothing of Himself, and gives life to whom He will in conformity with the Father's gift. But that relation is by no means parallel with the relation of other men who wrought miracles by Divine power, and must be taken in conjunction with the teaching of chapter v.; for He has the consciousness of unbroken communion with the Father, and of continual fulfilment of His will.

The prayer of thanksgiving, then, was spoken in order that the bystanders might, by hearing it, and seeing the miracle that followed, be led to recognise the true import of the miracle as a sign that He was sent from God. The prayer was a solemn appeal to God, a confident assumption of what was to follow. If it did follow, the appeal was effectual and the conclusion plain.

IV. Jesus and the living dead; the life-giving word. —The actual miracle is briefly told, but with unsurpassable vividness and solemnity. The brief emotion showed the Son of Man, but, as is always the case, the tokens of His humiliation lie side by side with those of His glory. The same voice that had sobbed in human grief now spoke in Divine power. Curt and authoritative is its utterance. He named the man, who still lived. The man heard, wherever he was, and dull as his ear was to sisters' weeping and all earthly noises. Wherever he was, he was not out of reach of Christ's will, and that voice could pierce the depths of the unseen world; Christ's commands run through the universe. The mere words were breath, but the will was mighty. Who is He whose bare will has power over material existences, and can shoot out its behests wherever there are creatures?

Who could paint that picture of the swathed form stumbling from the tomb, bound hand and foot, and the unaccustomed eyes shrinking from the sunlight, which had grown strange to them? What awe would await the taking away of the napkin from the face, and how the gazers would look to see what traces of the unseen world were there! But the reticence of the story is one of its charms. No eye is allowed to see the joy of the sisters or to peer into the home that night. "Loose him, and let him go." Christ's part is done. Other hands may undo the graveclothes; His will has loosed the grip of death.

LESSON XIV

What Jesus Thought about the Cross

St. John xii. 20-36

20. "And there were certain Greeks among them that came up to worship at the feast:

21. The same came therefore to Philip, which was of Bethsaida of Galilee, and desired him, saying, Sir, we would see Jesus.

22. Philip cometh and telleth Andrew: and again Andrew and Philip tell Jesus.

23. And Jesus answered them, saying, The hour is come, that the Son of man should be glorified.

24. Verily, verily, I say unto you, Except a corn of wheat fall into the ground and die, it abideth alone: but if it die, it bringeth forth much fruit.

25. He that loveth his life shall lose it; and he that hateth his life in this world shall keep it unto life eternal.

26. If any man serve Me, let him follow Me; and where I am, there shall also My servant be: if any man serve Me, him will My Father honour.

27. Now is My soul troubled; and what shall I say? Father, save Me from this hour: but for this cause came I unto this hour.

28. Father, glorify Thy name, Then came there a voice from heaven, saying, I have both glorified it, and will glorify it again.

29. The people therefore, that stood by, and heard it, said that it thundered: others said, An angel spake to Him.

30. Jesus answered and said, This voice came not because of Me, but for your sakes.

31. Now is the judgment of this world: now shall the prince of this world be cast out.

32. And I, if I be lifted up from the earth, will draw all men unto Me.

33. This He said, signifying what death He should die.

34. The people answered Him, We have heard out of the law that Christ abideth for ever: and how sayest Thou, The Son of man must be lifted up? who is this Son of man?

35. Then Jesus said unto them, Yet a little while is the light with you. Walk while ye have the light, lest darkness come upon you: for he that walketh in darkness knoweth not whither he goeth.

36. While ye have light, believe in the light, that ye may be the children of light. These things spake Jesus, and departed, and did hide Himself from them."

THE remarkable request of some Greek proselytes to see Jesus, interesting as it is, is but the starting-point of the great thoughts in this lesson. These carry the Evangelist so completely away that he does not tell us what came of the request. Jesus saw in it the first drops of the shower, the beginning of the Gentiles coming to His feet; and that prospect brought with it the vision of the death that must first be endured. The theme, then, of the lesson is what Jesus thought and felt about the Cross. "The place whereon thou standest is holy ground." We may note a difference in the tone of His words before and after the heavenly voice, and so take the whole as gathered into four parts.

I. The prevision of the near Cross, and the troubled soul of Jesus. The first emotion stirred by the request was triumph. "The hour is come, that the Son of Man should be glorified." Now, the subsequent context shows that the "glory" in view is chiefly that of His bringing men to Himself by His death, and that of the return to the pre-incarnate glory with the Father. But it is not to be forgotten that in this Gospel the Cross is always presented as the summit of Christ's glory, rather than as His lowest humiliation. It was His throne, because in it were most wondrously manifested the redeeming power and love which are the very flashing central light of all His brightness. In all His life we "behold His glory, . . . full of grace and truth"; but the rays are focussed there, where He hangs dying in the dark. There all paradoxes met. Shame is glory; weakness is strength; death is life.

Verses 24-26 point to the wide range of the same paradox of which the Cross is the crowning example. It

Less. XIV.] **What Jesus Thought about the Cross** 123

is seen in nature, where fruit is only possible by the destruction of the seed. No converts without martyrs, whether literally by actual death or by the daily dying of self-sacrifice. Life exemplifies the law. Eager clutching at the delights of natural life, and making it one's chief aim, is the sure way to lose all its sweetness and to miss the higher life, while the subordination, and, if needful, the sacrifice of "life in this world," leads straight to the possession of "life eternal." That was the truth for lack of which Greek literature, art, and glory rotted and perished. Discipleship demands the same conditions. Christ's servant must be Christ's follower on that road. The Cross must be his pattern as well as his trust. In a later part of this lesson (vers. 31, 32) the virtue of Christ's death, which has no parallel in the servant's "following," is stated; but here the possibility and necessity that discipleship shall be imitation even of that inimitable death are solemnly declared, with the appended blessed assurance that faithful following means final union and lowly service, a share in His honour and glory.

But swiftly a wave of agitation breaks upon the rock of His steadfast will. It is a true wave, but it breaks, and the rock is unshaken. Jesus had the natural, instinctive human recoil from death, and that clashed against the will to suffer. But it was His "soul," not His "spirit," which was "troubled." The hesitation so pathetically expressed here did not extend to His will, and was sinless. Whether we read the prayer "Save Me from this hour" as a question or as a definite petition, it seems to represent the one alternative of "what" He "should say," and is immediately superseded by the prayer in which the perturbed soul as well as the unmoved spirit unite. It is put aside, because Jesus sees the Cross as the great purpose of His coming, and so the very sight of the dreaded thing as the goal of His work gives strength to embrace it.

An old monkish painter makes the strengthening angel in Gethsemane hold forth a cross, and there is deep truth in the picture. The prayer, in which the whole man Jesus utters Himself, grasps the name "Father," and, in filial submission and trust, asks only that His name may be glorified. That is really a prayer that Jesus may die; but the pain is all lost in the contemplation of the issue, and so the universal pattern for true sons is set, and the victory in this prelude of Gethsemane is won. We can see but a little way into the depths of Christ's nature, and shall better use this tender and mysterious shrinking of human weakness overcome by filial submission and resolved sacrifice, if we adore the love that kept His will so firm, than if we curiously speculate beyond our depth.

II. We have the heavenly voice and how it sounded to dull ears (vers. 28, 29). The Revised Version gives "therefore" instead of "then" in verse 28 and thus brings out the significant connection of the voice with that prayer. Such prayer is sure of answer, and such filial surrender is sure of tokens of the Father's approval. If our prayers were more often like His, we should more often hear the voice following close upon them, and repeating in accents loud as thunder and sweet as an angel's speech our own low breathings turned into promises. As in the conspicuous humility of the baptism, and in the hour on the mountain when the mighty dead spake with Him of His decease, the Father's voice witnessed to Him. The past acts of glorifying are those of Christ's earthly ministry; the future are the declaring more gloriously of that name to the whole world by the Cross and subsequent triumph.

Every man hears in God's voice what he is fit to hear. Obviously there was an objective something, an audible sound. To the deafest there was a vague impression of some majestic noise from heaven, which said nothing, but was grand and meaningless as a thunder-clap. Others, a little more susceptible, caught something like articulate words, but discerned no significance, though they felt their sweetness and dignity, and so thought them an angel's voice. "Ye therefore hear them not, because ye are not of God." We can dull our ears till they will not even recognise God's voice as thunder, and, if it sounds meaningless to us, it is our own fault.

III. We have Christ's triumphant vision of the issues of the cross (vers. 30-33). Did Jesus not need the voice? His filial submission was perfect, and His assurance that His death was to glorify the Father's name was entire before it came. His words do not necessarily imply that He drew no strength from it, but only that His strengthening was not its main purpose. An absolute negative often in Scripture means a comparative one. But how could a voice be sent for people who did not understand it? Some of them would; and the deafness of men does not compel the dumbness of God. The revelation is given, and they who are capable receive it. Let us see that we do not make ourselves unfit to profit by what is sent for our sakes.

What did the voice teach its hearers? The true

meaning of Christ's past life, and of the great crisis now impending.

Jesus translates its lessons in the next words, which show Him, Victor over all the shrinking of flesh, triumphing in the world-wide and world-saving results of the Cross. He anticipates the rapidly approaching hour, and in the eagerness, if we may so say, of loving self-sacrifice, stretches out to meet the coming doom, in that prophetic and repeated "now." His death is the judgment of this world. Does not the fact of His death considered as the act of men reveal, as nothing else does, the depth of human alienation from God and goodness? If He thought of Himself only as a martyr, one among many, it was gross exaggeration to say that His death headed the black roll of the world's sins. On that hypothesis of His person, there have been many other deaths quite as criminal. Only the full-toned view of who and what the victim was warrants such a construction of the guilt of His slaying as is here.

Still more extravagant, on the supposition that Jesus is simply the best of men and teachers, is that other triumphant cry of victory over the defeated and cast-out "prince of this world." Only the full-toned view of the death of Christ as the sacrifice for the world's sins can warrant such a construction of its power to redeem the world from the tyranny of that usurper, and to dislodge him from his fortress. He and all his hosts hold their own, undisturbed by teachers and martyrs, but they flee before the power of the Cross of the Son of God, "who taketh away the sin of the world." He "made a show of them openly, triumphing over them in it."

The judgment and defeat are immediate results of the Cross, but the last issue, which Jesus stays Himself by beholding, is one that begins, indeed, contemporaneously with these, but stretches on through all time, and blesses each coming generation. Of course, the "lifting up" here is primarily a designation of the crucifixion (John iii. 14); but that is contemplated in connection with the other lifting up from the earth, in His ascension and session at the right hand of God. To draw men to Himself is the work of Christ till the end of the world. His magnet is the Cross. That drawing does not imply universal yielding to itself, for there may be resistance to it; but for evermore there stream out from that Cross powers which lay hold on hearts, and sweetly and mightily grapple them to Jesus. He Himself, and nothing less, is the centre; and what conquers men to be His, is His death.

Every form of so-called Christianity which weakens or obscures the sacrificial death of Jesus weakens the power of Christianity. A Christ without a cross is no match for the drawings of the world and its prince. This is the grand vision on His own death, in which Jesus found strength, and in which we shall find peace, pardon, and purity.

IV. We have the objection of the crowd, and Christ's last warnings to the nation. There must have been more spoken than is reported, or the people would not have puzzled about "the Son of man" being lifted up, since that title is not employed in the saying, though it occurs in verse 23. They knew that Jesus claimed to be the Messiah, and, building on passages which spoke of His kingdom as everlasting, they anticipated Messiah's permanent, miraculous life on earth. They have heard Jesus saying that "the Son of Man" is to be lifted up from the earth, and they supposed that He was speaking of Himself by that name; but, if so, what about His Messianic claims? They are in a fog, and are pottering about interpretations of the law, instead of letting the light, which was shining before them, shine into them.

Texts out of the Prophets were all very well, but, if they would open their eyes and their hearts to Him standing there before them, they would find all their pedantic difficulties melt away. The best way to deal with similar trivial objections sometimes is to press the positive revelation of Christ, and let that speak. So here Jesus does not "answer" the question, but speaks a solemn warning—His last words before the cross—to the nation. The time was short. In a few minutes He would go over Olivet to Bethany, only to return for the upper room and the cross. But still there was time.

Two exhortations are given, the former enforced by the misery of darkness, the latter by the blessings of transformation into light. The former counsels "walk while ye have the light." Progress in the knowledge of Him could yet be won. Action correspondent to the light was yet possible. So is it ever. And the solemn alternative is certain if we do not "walk." Darkness is, as it were, hurrying up behind, and only by diligent carrying out of Christ's precepts, and pressing towards fuller knowledge, can we escape it. If it fall on us, we shall wander without guide or clear aim, and be lost in the desert. The history of Israel ever since is a commentary on the words, as it strays through the world with no aim or hope beyond earth. They are a parable and warning for us.

But Jesus will not let His last word be a threat. Therefore, in still clearer tones, He speaks a merciful invitation and a glorious promise. Believe on the light, is His invitation to us all. And the gracious hope is offered to each, of becoming, by faith, changed into the substance of that to which we trust, and having all our darkness of sorrow, ignorance, and sin turned into light in the Lord. So some poor wreath of cold, wet mist, lying near the rising sun, is suffused with light in all its dank depths, and glows with radiant hues caught from the great light near which it hangs.

LESSON XV

The Master-Servant

St. John xiii. 1-17.

1. "Now before the feast of the passover, when Jesus knew that His hour was come that He should depart out of this world unto the Father, having loved His own which were in the world, He loved them unto the end.

2. And supper being ended, the devil having now put into the heart of Judas Iscariot, Simon's son, to betray Him;

3. Jesus knowing that the Father had given all things into His hands, and that He was come from God, and went to God;

4. He riseth from supper, and laid aside His garments; and took a towel, and girded Himself.

5. After that He poureth water into a bason, and began to wash the disciples' feet, and to wipe them with the towel wherewith He was girded.

6. Then cometh He to Simon Peter: and Peter saith unto Him, Lord, dost Thou wash my feet?

7. Jesus answered and said unto him, What I do thou knowest not now; but thou shalt know hereafter.

8. Peter saith unto Him, Thou shalt never wash my feet. Jesus answered him, If I wash thee not, thou hast no part with Me.

9. Simon Peter saith unto Him, Lord, not my feet only, but also my hands and my head.

10. Jesus saith to him, He that is washed needeth not save to wash his feet, but is clean every whit: and ye are clean, but not all.

11. For He knew who should betray Him; therefore said He, Ye are not all clean.

12. So after He had washed their feet, and had taken His garments, and was set down again, He said unto them, Know ye what I have done to you?

13. Ye call me Master and Lord: and ye say well; for so I am.

14. If I then, your Lord and Master, have washed your feet; ye also ought to wash one another's feet.

15. For I have given you an example, that ye should do as I have done to you.

16. Verily, verily, I say unto you, The servant is not greater than his lord; neither he that is sent greater than he that sent him.

17. If ye know these things, happy are ye if ye do them."

IN this lesson we have four stages,—the glimpse into the heart of Jesus, and the impelling motives to the great act of tender humility; that act itself described in all the details of its lowliness; the episode of the misplaced and spurious humility which was really arrogance; and the application, by the Master and Lord, of the lesson which He taught in the form of a servant.

I. Verse 1 should be regarded as an introduction, not only to the one act of foot-washing, but to the whole following section, including all the sacred teachings of the upper room. It is best to adopt the marginal rendering of "to the uttermost"; for John is more concerned to tell us how, at that supreme moment, Christ's love shone forth as absolutely perfect, than simply to assure us of its continuance. So understanding the last clause of the verse, its former part becomes an explanation of the influences which gave rise to the special manifestations of that love in the succeeding acts, discourses, and prayer. When, then, are these influences?

First, the consciousness that separation was at hand. We have heard much about "His hour" in this Gospel. His unbroken communion with the Father taught Him the duty proper to each moment, and He never acted without the illuminating assurance that it was the time to act. But now the supreme hour was close at hand. For what? The language is remarkable,—"that He should depart out of this world unto the Father."

Then His death was voluntary and His own act, as it is ever represented in this Gospel. He is not cast out of the world by others, but departs. He goes, not to the grave, but "to the Father." So may death be to us, if we are His.

This consciousness increased the manifestations of His love. We, too, know that parting brings deeper tenderness, as an earthquake may lay bare hidden veins of gold. The heart crowds all its love into a look or a word or an embrace which two may find it life to remember. Blessed is it to know that Jesus felt the same, and sought to make the last moments tender moments, for His sake as well as for ours. But it was more than human love which so forgot His own sufferings in the desire to pour itself into the hearts that were soon to be stricken and solitary.

That love, too, was one which owned the obligation created by its own past. "Having loved, ... He loved." Alas, how much human love has the opposite for its epitaph, "Having loved, ... he tired of loving"! But Christ's past is the pledge of His future, and every "has" of His holds a "will" in its hand. Even earthly love may sometimes have in its depth the guarantee that it is not "born for death"; but how much more Christ's, which is, as He is, the same yesterday, and to-day, and for ever! That love clasps "its own" with special tenderness, and it is moved to pour itself out over those who trust Him, with such specialty because He knows their dangers, left to fight and be tempted "in the world."

Verses 2 and 3, in similar fashion, give the precise date and the impelling motives of the foot-washing. The time was "during supper" (Rev. Ver.), at what point in the meal we are not told, and need not try to guess. Possibly, as has been thought, the usual washing of the guests' feet had been omitted at the beginning of the meal, and the dispute as to who was greatest may have been connected with that omission. But that is uncertain. Why is the treachery of Judas brought into prominence at this point ? Probably to enhance the lowly forbearance which washed even his feet, as well as to explain the allusions to him in what follows, and to suggest that Jesus read his heart, and saw, in its black resolve, the token that His hour was come.

At that hour of clearly discerned nearness to the cross, Jesus was unhesitatingly conscious of universal authority, of His pre-incarnate glory and mission, and of His return to the Father. That consciousness must be taken along with the motives in verse 1, and then we learn that the lowliness of Jesus, when He stooped to be a servant, was based on His knowing himself Divine and on His infinite love. Not *although*, but *because*, He was conscious of Divine authority, origin, and destination, did He humble Himself thus. What a strange "therefore" it is in the world's eyes !

II. Verses 4 and 5 give with awe-struck particularity the marvellous details of the fact, which had left an ineffaceable impression on the disciple who reclined next the Lord at the table, and which now come all back to him, step by step, with yet deeper sense of their wonder and meaning. We can see the little company startled by His rising, and watching in silence each successive detail. The task was that of a slave, or, at least, of the lowest in rank of those present. The disciples had had a hot journey from Bethany, and, no doubt, needed the service. No part of the servile task did He omit, not even the indignity of divesting Himself of His upper robe, and wrapping round Him the slave's towel; Himself filled the bason that stood ready, and thought nothing unworthy, even to wiping the wet feet with the towel which touched His own body.

Well may the Evangelist linger over such a deed, and well may we try to print deep on our hearts its graciousness and stringent exhortation to us. But while the deed was in itself the most touching manifestation of the tender emotions that then filled Christ's heart, and loses its supreme beauty unless we think of it as the spontaneous outgush of His love, we can scarcely fail to note how it symbolises His whole work, or, rather, how it shows the same principles at work on a lower plane, which find their highest manifestation in His incarnation and life of service. He rose from His place in the uncreated glory. He divested Himself of the robes of His Divine majesty. He assumed the form of a servant, and girded Himself with the slave's badge. He filled the bason, providing the means of cleansing. He applied the cleansing water. Alone He originated, prepared for, effected, carried out, and completed the work. "Himself doing all things with all alacrity."

III. Verses 6-11 give the ill-timed humility of Peter, which was really presumption with a mask on. The language of verse 6 implies that others had been washed before Peter; but his impetuous love, his strong self-will, and his liking for being unlike the others, burst out in the remonstrance. He had thought that he knew better than Christ before now, and he was always ready with his advice. No doubt his question came from the sense of his own inferiority, as is marked by the emphatic pronouns "Thou" and "I." But an adequate sense of it would have taught him that Christ could not degrade Himself, however low He stooped, and that he,

Peter, could not be unworthy to receive anything which Jesus chose to give.

The gentle answer, which repressed rashness by impressing present ignorance and promising future knowledge, may teach us all how perilous it is to make ourselves the judges of what is becoming to a Divine love dealing with sinful men. The partial explanation immediately following can scarcely be what Jesus meant by the promise of knowledge hereafter; for "after these things" seems to stretch to all the incidents of the passion on which He was now entering, and the time of illumination, when all the significance should be plain, was years ahead.

But rash self-will is not to be repressed by considerations of its ignorance, and forbearance may only make it bolder. The comparatively modest question changed into obstinate, rude refusal. "Never" is opposed to "hereafter," as if he said, "I do not care what the future may teach me, which I do not know now; but I know this, that no future can teach me to let Thee do such a thing to me." It was a flat contradiction of Christ, and assumed superior knowledge to His. It strained the tie of discipleship to almost breaking-point. So closely does "voluntary humility" neighbour arrogant self-assertion and pride; so dangerous is it to suppose ourselves too lowly for Jesus to stoop to serve and cleanse us.

Christ's answer has a tone of sternness in its plain statement of what was involved. Peter had said "never," and Jesus accepts the word, and probes the speaker's heart, to see if he will stand by his refusal when he knows that it means losing all share in Him. It is usually said by commentators now that the context forbids any direct reference to the forgiveness of sins, and limits the meaning of the solemn words to a declaration that separation must follow the want of submission. But the reference to forgiveness and cleansing from sin is undeniable in verse 10, and it seems most natural to see it here also. If Jesus is not our Saviour from the guilt and power of sin, we have no vital union with Him. He must be that or nothing; and the converse is also true, that, if He is anything to us, He will cleanse us.

The prospect of separation from the Lord whom he loved so deeply brings the wayward, true-hearted disciple back to lowliness and a passion of clinging affection. These quick revulsions, all so genuine and so whole-souled, give a charm to Peter which the others lack. "If washing means union with Thee, and what is unwashed is parted from Thee, let my whole self be blessed with it." It is the vehement cry of the soul longing for union with Jesus. Does it wake an echo in ours? If we have any real love for that Lord, it will. It will, if we have any deep sense of our own sin, and consciousness that it makes separation. One film of sin is a thicker barrier than would be made if the space from this spot to His throne were covered with solid wall.

Jesus answers the request, which went as much too far on the one side as the refusal did on the other, by great words, capable of such wide application, and throwing light on the whole teaching of Scripture as to sanctification. There is an initial cleansing of the whole man, comparable to the entire bathing of the body. That corresponds to the entire forgiveness and ideally complete cleansing by the impartation of the new nature, which is given in the initial act of faith. But the ways of the world are foul, and bare or sandalled feet on dusty or muddy roads are stained by travel. So the cleansed spirit has yet to avail itself of continual fresh resort to the blood of cleansing, and daily to pray for pardon as for daily bread. So the lessons of the whole episode are: No Christ for us unless He cleanse; no cleansing for us unless from Christ; no cleansing without faith, and daily cleansing for stains contracted even by cleansed men.

IV. Verses 12-17 give the application of the pattern to ourselves. We note the remarkable juxtaposition of humility and loftiness. Seated again at table, Jesus declares His supreme authority as Teacher of truth and Ruler of life in uncompromising tones. No man ever rendered Him higher honour or titles than He accepted as His right. The mystery of the Master-Servant, unapproachable as it is, has yet an imitable side; and in that most pathetic and wonderful incident Jesus sets forth the law for all His followers. That law is that dignity binds to service. If we are Christ's, we must stoop to serve, and serve to cleanse. The noblest form of help is to help men to get rid of their sin. The highest glory of powers and gifts is to humble oneself for the lowest, and to be ready to be a slave, if we may wash any stained soul or bind any bleeding feet.

The example of Christ includes what He has done for us. Some of us are willing to look to the Cross as the foundation of our hope, who are not willing to take it as the law of our lives. But the benefits of the gospel are meant to impel us to corresponding action. How little any of us have caught the whole sweep of the meaning of that imperative "example, that ye should do as I have done to you." What have we received from Him? What have we given to men? Are we not too much like some sullen, land-locked lake, which receives many streams and gives forth none? If our acts to others are not widened to correspond to Christ's to and for us, the reverse process will set in, and Christ's acts and gifts to us will shrink to the narrowness of ours to others.

We all know that He is our example, and that even in the supreme and unapproachable gift of His death we ought to find the model for our lives. But the gulf between knowledge and practice is all too wide, and so our Lord adds one more to the Beatitudes, pronouncing those blessed who add doing to knowing. Only they really know who translate all their knowledge into performance. Only they are truly blessed who have no principles which do not regulate conduct, and no conduct which is not regulated by principle. The one principle which can shape all life into blessedness is, Do as Jesus has done for you. Stoop that you may serve, and let your service be cleansing.

LESSON XVI

The Present-Absent Christ and the Abiding Comforter

ST. JOHN xiv. 1-3, 15-27

1. "Let not your heart be troubled: ye believe in God, believe also in Me.
2. In My Father's house are many mansions: if it were not so, I would have told you. I go to prepare a place for you.
3. And if I go and prepare a place for you, I will come again, and receive you unto Myself; that where I am, there ye may be also. . . .
15. If ye love Me, keep My commandments.
16. And I will pray the Father, and He shall give you another Comforter, that He may abide with you for ever;
17. Even the Spirit of truth; whom the world cannot receive, because it seeth Him not, neither knoweth Him: but ye know Him; for He dwelleth with you, and shall be in you.
18. I will not leave you comfortless: I will come to you.
19. Yet a little while, and the world seeth Me no more; but ye see Me: because I live, ye shall live also.
20. At that day ye shall know that I am in My Father, and ye in Me, and I in you.
21. He that hath My commandments, and keepeth them, He it is that loveth Me: and he that loveth Me shall be loved of My Father, and I will love Him, and will manifest Myself to Him.
22. Judas saith unto Him, not Iscariot, Lord, how is it that Thou wilt manifest Thyself unto us, and not unto the world?
23. Jesus answered and said unto him, If a man love Me, he will keep My words: and My Father will love him, and we will come unto him, and make our abode with him
24. He that loveth Me not keepeth not My sayings: and the word which ye hear is not Mine, but the Father's which sent Me.
25. These things have I spoken unto you, being yet present with you.
26. But the Comforter, which is the Holy Ghost, whom the Father will send in My name, He shall teach you all things, and bring all things to your remembrance, whatsoever I have said unto you.
27. Peace I leave with you, My peace I give unto you: not as the world giveth, give I unto you. Let not your heart be troubled, neither let it be afraid."

THE depth, sweetness, and calm of these wonderful words in the upper room lift them high above comment. Who can reproduce their tender music, or exhaust their deep meaning? We can but skim the surface.

I. The first three verses apply the simplest and most sufficient soothing to the sorrow for His departure. In verse 1 the exhortation to twofold and yet single trust presents faith in God, which is also faith in Jesus, as the one antidote to trouble of heart. What is the use of telling men not to be troubled, unless you can show them how? How else can coiling sorrow be cast out than by faith? Jesus asks the same trust which we give to God, and these two are one. He does not bid us ruin our faith by dividing it between two objects. Strange words from a Man who was within twenty-four hours of death!

Verse 2 clothes great truths in simple words, and changes the aspect of departure by the revelation of the place whither He goes, and of the share they had in His going, and appeals to His frankness in telling them the sad tidings, as assuring them that He would not have hidden it from them if His departure had been parting. It is really the preparation for their eternal reunion. "My Father's house. . . . Wist ye not that there is My place?" Heaven is the true temple, and in it is room for these eleven poor men, and for millions more. The places there are "mansions," perpetual abodes. Unchangeableness and repose breathe from the word. Jesus tells us all that we need, though less than we sometimes wish. If there were any dismal separation, any dark shadow brooding over that future, He would not leave us to find it out too late. We may utterly trust His absolute frankness, and be content to know that the gaps in our knowledge hide nothing terrible, or affecting permanent repose in and with Him in the Father's house.

Verse 3 opens the blessed prospect of return and reunion. How He prepares the place we know not, nor need to know. Perhaps, if He had not gone thither in human form, there had been no place. Certainly, if He stood not before the throne, we could never stand there. Only because the Lamb is "in the midst of the throne," can the elders, the representatives of redeemed manhood, "adore around."

II. Verses 15-17 are mainly occupied with the promise of the Comforter. They present to our thoughts the loving obedience which secures the Saviour's intercession, the praying Christ, the giving Father, and the abiding Spirit. Hitherto "believe" has been the keyword. Now it is "love." Jesus has just promised to do whatsoever we ask in His name. Now He bids us do whatsoever He commands. On both sides is love set in motion by a message from the other. His love commands, and delights to be asked. Ours should ask, and delight to be commanded. Verse 15 contains the all-sufficient guide for life. His "commandments" are Himself. That pattern is enough for conduct, for character, and for all perplexities. Here is the all-powerful motive. "Ye will keep," says the Revised Version. Love will have power to sway life. It is the foundation of obedience, and obedience is its sure outcome. All the emotional, mystic, and select experiences of Christians must submit to this plain test: Do they help to obedience?

The root of such active love is "believe," and its issues are next unfolded. "I will pray, . . . and He will give." His intercession is our hope. It is His present work. His presence within the veil, His continual presenting of His finished work as the reason for blessing being given to us, are truths of which we can but grasp part; but without them the Cross would lack its meaning and be shorn of its power. Jesus is sure of answer to His prayer.

The one all-inclusive gift secured by Christ's intercession is "the Comforter." We probably know that that name has shrunk in significance in our modern English, and that it means, and was understood at the date of the earlier translations to mean, more than it now does. It is wider than "consoler," meaning literally "one called to aid another," and so covering the meanings of "advocate," "helper," "strengthener," "guide," and "instructor." By whatever processes a man can be made strong, these are the Spirit's work. This Advocate is to replace Christ, and carry on His work. He is "another Comforter," and is to be an abiding presence, not going away, as Jesus was about to do. But mark how He will do His work. He is "the Spirit of truth." Not that He brings new truth,—that is Christ's work,—but the Spirit has for His weapon and source of strength the revelation summed and finished in Christ's person and work.

The world—that is, the aggregate of men considered as separated from God and immersed in the material—cannot have this Strengthener, any more than low, sensuous natures are capable of perceiving the highest forms of natural beauty or of art. Of course, the "conviction" which the Spirit works on "the world" is not the matter in hand here. But men put out their eyes by sin and worldly lusts, and cannot see what purer vision suns itself in beholding. Some men need oculists, not light. The world cannot receive, because it does not know. The disciples know, because they receive. Possession and knowledge are mutual cause and effect; or perhaps, rather, they are one and the same thing. Even at that hour the Spirit abode with the disciples, for He was in Christ; but the future was to bring a clearer, closer knowledge and possession, when, after Pentecost, He should not only be with, but in, them. These great promises are for all Christian souls to the end. The way to the personal experience of their sweet truth is, as this discourse shows, first, "believe"; then, "love"; then, "do His commandments."

III. Verses 18-21 carry the comfort of the sorrowing disciples still further, by assuring them that Christ Himself will come to them, and give them greater gifts than they could ever possess otherwise. Reunion, influence from afar, the preparation of a place, were not all that they craved for. So there are, in verses 18 and 19, three paradoxes: the absent Christ is present; the unseen Christ is visible; the dying Christ is life-giving. The word rendered "comfortless" (ver. 18) is "orphans." The forlorn disciples would be like fatherless and motherless children without Him, and nothing would keep them from being so but His presence. Unless Christ be with us, we are desolate.

He does not say "I will come," but "I come,"—an immediately impending coming. If His future coming were meant, then till then all His people are to be as orphans; and that cannot be. There is a coming, then, contemporaneous with His bodily absence. "Bodily" is not a synonym for "real." He came in the very act of going. Being absent, He is present with us, if we will. How the vivid belief in Christ's real presence would calm, glorify, and hallow life! Again, the unseen Christ is a seen Christ. "Yet a little while" is best interpreted as covering all the time till the ascension, and the brief appearances during the forty days are too little to be the fulfilment of this promise, which necessarily has the same extension in time as the coming—that is, is continuous and permanent.

"See," when denied as to the world, means bodily sight; when promise to disciples, spiritual perception. Every Christian life may be blessed with the vision of the present Christ. "See" is a strong word, implying very vivid, direct, and certain knowledge and consciousness. Is Jesus so near us, and are we so aware and sure of Him, that the sight of sense is less than that of spirit? Again, the dying Christ lives and gives life. "I live" is a timeless present tense, all but identical with "Jehovah." We live because, and therefore, as long as, and, in a true correspondence, in the same manner as He lives. We can never die as long as the eternally "living who became dead" is alive, and that is "for evermore."

Verse 20 discloses the blessed consequence of His coming. Because the disciple has Christ's presence, sees Him and draws kindred life from Him, he will know by experience Christ's indwelling at once in the Father and in His servant, and His servant's indwelling in Him. "That day" is the whole period between ascension and return in bodily form. In that period the experiences just promised will be the best teachers of fundamental Christian truth. But how can the relation between Father and Son ever have any verification in ourselves? If these preceding promises be fulfilled to me, my experiences will be such as to be inexplicable, except on the supposition of their having a Divine source. They bear the signature of a Divine hand. I know that it is Jesus who gives them, and that He could not give them unless He was in the Father. Similarly, the consciousness of Christ present, seen, life-giving, carries the knowledge that Jesus is in us; for we feel His touch, and we are in Him; for we are aware of the power that encompasses us and the atmosphere in which we have our being.

Verse 21 closes the first section of the discourse. Its first words are substantially equivalent to verse 15, but the slight difference is significant. The former saying begins with the root, and works outward to the fruit; while this verse takes the reverse order, beginning with the fruit and going inwards to the root. Note that "hath My commandments." The only real possession of them is in the heart. Practical obedience is the test of love. The emphatic "he" and the order of the sentence, putting the fruits first, give it a sharp edge as against false pretensions. Christ stamps with His hall-mark as gold no mere emotion, however genuine and passionate, but only that which issues in Christian conduct and character.

Such love is rewarded by further and sweeter gifts of Divine love and manifestation. What boldness in saying that, if a man loves Christ, God will love him!

Of course, that saying does not begin at the very beginning. "We love Him because He first loved us" digs a story deeper down in the building. What is in hand is, not how a man comes to receive the love of God at first, but how a Christian grows in possession of it. God loves all men, but the heart that believes and therefore loves, and loves and therefore obeys, will receive deeper and sweeter tokens of God's love. Further, Christ will meet us on the path of obedience, with more and more of His love unveiled to our eyes.

IV. In verses 22-24, Judas' question gives occasion for a statement of the conditions of Christ's self-manifestation, both positively and negatively. The question is that of a listener dimly understanding Jesus, perceiving that the public display which had seemed coming, when Christ rode into Jerusalem, was somehow not to be. "What is come to pass that?" etc. He understands that somehow "unto us, and not unto the world," is the revelation to be made. Christ answers both parts of the question, and tells us what brings Christ and what Christ brings, and then what keeps away Him and His gifts. Note the width of the words "if a man," instead of "if ye" (ver. 15), thus telling Judas that his complacent assumption, "unto us," was a narrow reading of the sweep of the promise.

We have already seen what brings Christ, and need only here note that the test of love is said to be keeping Christ's "word," which suggests that not only His commandments, but all His words, are to be treasured, and, further, that His many words are one whole, and, further, that every word of His holds some law for practical life in its depths. Obedience brings the sense of the Father's love, and the reality of His abiding presence, which is also Christ's presence. How close must be that union of Father and Son whereby Jesus could dare to say, "We will come"! How blessed the dwelling of the Divine guest, which is permanent, as long as the obedience which is its condition endures! The negative side shows what keeps away Jesus. Unloving disobedience closes the heart. Two principles are laid down. First, no love, no obedience. Second, disobedience to Christ is disobedience to God. Jesus is sure that all He speaks is God's word. What should we think of a religious teacher who began by saying, "Remember that everything which I say God says"? The conclusion is not stated, but easily drawn. Unloving obedience, then, will keep away Christ, and in Him God. It is possible, then, not to see Christ, though He stands beside us. The simple absence of love is fatal.

V. A slight pause in the flow of speech seems to come in, and then in verses 25 and 26 Jesus looks back on what He has said, and contrasts His teaching with that future teaching by the Comforter, whom He has already, in a different connection, promised. Mark the name here given to the Teacher-Spirit. His office of Strengthener is brought into immediate connection with His teaching; for what can more fully equip us with power from on high than the firm grasp of the truth as it is in Jesus? That Teacher is, further, "the Holy Ghost." That name in this connection suggests that there is no holiness without such knowledge, and no learning of the truth without holiness. This Teacher-Spirit is "sent in Christ's name." In some deep sense

God acts as representing Christ, and it is on the historic manifestation of Christ as basis that the Spirit is sent. Revelation must be complete before He who came to unfold and impress it had material to work with. Mark, too, the unmistakable declaration of the personality of the Spirit: "He shall teach." That cannot be said of an influence.

The lesson-book of the Teacher-Spirit is clearly set forth as Christ, "all things whatsoever I have said." Jesus Himself contrasts here the partial understanding of His words while on earth with the fuller grasp of their inexhaustible meaning to be attained hereafter. His words can never be fathomed, much less exhausted. The Spirit is ever with His Church, teaching each age to understand some little bit more of their depth. True progress consists, not in getting beyond Jesus, but in getting more deeply into His ever-fresh truth. The problems of this generation will find their solution where those of past generations have found theirs, and the old commandment of the old Christ will be the new commandment of the new Christ. As long as we have an abiding Spirit to teach the endless fulness of His words to loving obedience, we need not fear, though the things which can be shaken are removed. The world will not outgrow Jesus Christ. All change will but make more plain His inexhaustibleness, and reveal new treasures in His familiar and enduring words.

LESSON XVII

The Vine and the Branches

St. John xv. 1-16

1. "I am the true vine, and My Father is the husbandman.

2. Every branch in Me that beareth not fruit He taketh away: and every branch that beareth fruit, He purgeth it, that it may bring forth more fruit.

3. Now ye are clean through the word which I have spoken unto you.

4. Abide in Me, and I in you. As the branch cannot bear fruit of itself, except it abide in the vine; no more can ye, except ye abide in Me.

5. I am the vine, ye are the branches: He that abideth in Me, and I in him, the same bringeth forth much fruit: for without Me ye can do nothing.

6. If a man abide not in Me, he is cast forth as a branch, and is withered; and men gather them, and cast them into the fire, and they are burned.

7. If ye abide in Me, and My words abide in you, ye shall ask what ye will, and it shall be done unto you.

8. Herein is My Father glorified, that ye bear much fruit; so shall ye be My disciples.

9. As the Father hath loved Me, so have I loved you: continue ye in My love.

10. If ye keep My commandments, ye shall abide in My love; even as I have kept My Father's commandments, and abide in His love.

11. These things have I spoken unto you, that My joy might remain in you, and that your joy might be full.

12. This is My commandment, That ye love one another, as I have loved you.

13. Greater love hath no man than this, that a man lay down his life for his friends.

14. Ye are My friends, if ye do whatsoever I command you.

15. Henceforth I call you not servants; for the servant knoweth not what his Lord doeth: but I have called you friends; for all things that I have heard of My Father I have made known unto you.

16. Ye have not chosen Me, but I have chosen you, and ordained you, that ye should go and bring forth fruit, and that your fruit should remain; that whatsoever ye shall ask of the Father in My name, He may give it you."

THE last words of the fourteenth chapter show that there is a slight break in the discourse, and possibly a change of place. Many guesses have been made as to the occasion suggesting the parable of our lesson; but these are unimportant. A vine by the wayside, or the golden vine on the temple doors, or the "fruit of the vine" which had just been used for the Lord's Supper, may have shaped the allusion.

I. The lovely and significant parable occupies verses 1-8. It falls into two halves, of which the first (vers. 1-4) gives the image in its most general aspect, and the second (vers. 5-8) dwells on the branches abiding in the vine, and the solemn issues involved. Jesus is the "true Vine," the reality of which the material one to which He perhaps pointed is but a shadow, and of which Israel had failed to be the spiritual emblem which it was meant to be. One life fills the plant from root through stem, and reddens and mellows each cluster. So His life pervades all His true followers; and that one life results in oneness of relation to God, of character, and of destiny. We are sons of God in Him, lights of the world by Him, clothed with His righteousness, sanctified by His Spirit, and at last with Him and glorified with His glory.

The husbandman and his dressing of the vine comes next. Christ is usually presented as the Cultivator, but the form of the parable requires that here the Father, who, however, works through the Son, should do that office. The vinedresser's chief tool is a knife. Pruning looks merciless and wasteful, but it is done scientifically, without random strokes. Nothing is cut away except that which it is gain to lose. Dead wood has to be cut out, and living wood has to be cut back. The whole strain of the parable implies that life, however imperfect, will produce some fruit, and therefore leads to the conclusion that the utterly fruitless branches are people with a merely nominal connection with Christ, whose "taking away" is simply making visible the fact that they are not His at all.

But pruning is needed by true branches, for we all have two natures if we are in Christ, and the one flourishes at the other's expense; therefore the Husbandman has to cut the rank shoots from self, that all our force may be thrown into growing fruit. Then we have the condition of fruitfulness laid down as abiding in Christ. There may be much work and no fruit. What we bring forth "of ourselves" is no more fruit than cankers are roses. The reception of the life which secures fruit depends on our own effort. We have to take pains that we may abide in Christ, and so secure His abiding in us. If a canal lock be empty, the water will press on it, and open the gates, and fill it. If we empty the heart, Christ will come in. If we abide in Him, by thought, love, desire, by submission and reference of all work to Him, He will dwell in us, and we shall be fruitful branches.

Verses 5-8 repeat, but with additions, these truths. Christ was not afraid of repetition. He broke the bread of life small, and fed the disciples little and often. In these four verses are four aspects of the great truth of union with Him. First, the fruitfulness of union. Note the pointed application of the truth, "*Ye* are the branches." Toothless generalities are useless; there must be a driving home of truth to the individual. The great condition of fruit-bearing is quiet abiding in Christ,—a temper far remote from noise and bustle. We must be much within the veil, and have still hearts; and the harder our work, the more must we "labour to enter into that rest."

Mark the promise of "much fruit." Why do we bear a shrivelled cluster or two, more like marbles than grapes? Because we do not abide in Him. Christ puts but two alternatives,—no fruit or much. The average crop nowadays is "little." "Apart from Me, nothing," is the emphatic statement here. Life without Jesus is a long sum, which, added up, has for its total a cipher.

Second, the converse truth is stated, that separation means withering and destruction. How the leaves shrivel on a plucked branch! So, separate from Christ, men wither and Churches droop. Withering brings destruction. The language describes what befalls actual branches in literal vines, but is symbolic of the fate of men apart from Jesus. Note the mysterious language: "They gather." Who do? and who cast into the fire? All is left in unexplained awfulness. Enough to know that to be in the Vine or thrown into the fire are the alternatives. Once more, union with Christ brings satisfaction of desires. If He, by His words, abide in us, and we in Him, our "will" harmonises with His, and we get our wishes when they are moulded by His indwelling word.

Once more, union with Him leads to God's glorifying and our increasing discipleship. Do we so live that the sight of us kindles sweeter and worthier thoughts of God in men? Thus abiding, we shall "become" (as the accurate rendering is) His disciples. We never, on earth, reach full discipleship, but should be ever in process of becoming His true servants. The fruit borne by union with Him will help us nearer to Him.

II. Verses 9-11 are a kind of conclusion of the parable, presenting a somewhat different aspect of its main drift, and telling us His purpose in it. Three things are spoken of in these verses as abiding,—love, obedience, joy. The abiding is, first, abiding in love. Christ claims to be in an altogether unique manner the object of the Father's love, and—no less wonderful—to be able to love like the Father,—as deeply, purely, fully, eternally, and with all the unnamable perfectness of Divine love. In that mysterious, tender, perfect love He bids us abide,—meaning thereby, not the continuance of our emotion of love to Him, but our keeping ourselves in the sacred precincts of His love to us. That abiding is in our own power. The dwellers in the clefts of that riven Rock need no other defence.

The second abiding thing is obedience, by which we abide in the love of Christ. Fruit is grown without effort, but the human side of the truth is more prominent here, where the converse of the previous thought is set forth; namely, that obedience is the condition of abiding. Jesus does not say "Obey God as I have done, and He will love you," but "Obey Me as I obey Him, and I will love you." Who is He that thus comes between us and God? And does He come between, or rather lead us to the Father? He does love us the better the more we do His will. That love which sought the wandering sheep will pour itself more tenderly on it when it follows close at the heels of the Shepherd.

The third abiding thing is joy, if the reading of the Authorised Version be retained. This was a strange time for Jesus to speak of His joy, with Gethsemane and Calvary so near. Was the Man of Sorrows a joyful man? He was anointed with the oil of gladness above His fellows, because He absolutely surrendered Himself to the Father's will; and that joy He will give us if we too give up ourselves at the bidding of love. Such joy will be progressive, ever full, and ever advancing towards fuller possession of His joys.

III. Verses twelve and thirteen pass from the relation of branches to vine to that of branches to each other, of which the natural expression is mutual love. The commandments are all summed in one—love. Then love is obligatory. But can it be produced to order? Commandment and love do not go well together, but yet much may be done to cultivate it. Christians should feel nearer to each other, however unlike in temperament, culture, and position, than they are to non-Christians to whom in these respects they may be most like. If this be the sum of His commandments, it must be the essence of our duty, and hold every other right feeling and deed in germ in itself. When Jesus was about to leave His little flock, He did not talk to them about institutions, Church order, and the like, but gave this one all-sufficient injunction. If that be right, everything will come right.

Further, He here gives the pattern and measure of mutual love. He had just declared that His love was like God's, and now He bids us make ours like His. Think of a man calmly saying, "I am the embodiment of perfect love, the pattern for all hearts." But still more remarkable is it that He sets before us His death as our pattern, not, indeed, in its propitiatory character, but as being a voluntary, love-impelled surrender for our good. That is the model for us,—a solemn thought which may well bring a blush to our cheeks and penitence to our consciences. "For His friends." But He died for enemies, that He might make them friends. The word here does not mean those who loved Him, but those whom He loved, and so refers to the same persons as Paul had in view in his variation of this saying, and called "enemies."

IV. The closing verses of the lesson describe Christ's friends. They tell us what His friends do for Him, what He does for them, how they come to be so. "Friends" here means mainly those who love Him, and Jesus here stoops to accept and rejoice in the imperfect love of these poor men and of us. But the singular blending of friendship and authority is noticeable. He commands, though He is Friend; He is Friend, though He commands. So we should cherish at once absolute submission and closest friendship. Obedience will knit the tie between Him and us more closely; and the closer tie will give clearer insight into His will, and fuller joy in doing it.

Verse fifteen tells us what Christ does for His friends. The slave may see what his lord does, but does not know his purpose or motive, and so cannot estimate his acts. A servant in his master's confidence is something more than a servant. But Jesus calls His disciples "friends," and had called them so in act before He here named them so. Jesus recognises the obligation of perfect frankness, and He will tell His friends everything that He can. Of course, that frankness has its limits in the power of reception in the hearers; for He does not pour His treasures into vessels that will spill them, and there were many things yet to be spoken which remained unspoken "because ye cannot carry them now." That frankness continues, and to-day we, if we listen to Him, may know all which it concerns us to know, and may peacefully acquiesce in ignorance about much which we sometimes feel we wish to know. Let us be certain that we have caught all the words which He has spoken. That still small voice is not heard amid the babble of earth and the cries of our own hearts; but if we keep silent before the Lord, it will fill the silence with music.

Then we have, in verse sixteen, how and why Christ's friends come to be so. The reference is primarily to the apostles, chosen and ordained to their office, and in their apostolic labours bringing forth abiding fruit. But the saying has a far wider application. The beginning of all friendship between Christ and men lies with Him. I suppose that every man who has felt Christ's love will say, whatever his theological standpoint, "I was apprehended of Christ." It is because He lays His seeking hand upon us that we come to Him, and His choice of us precedes ours of Him.

This is how men come to be His friends, because, when they were enemies, He gave Himself for them, and has ever since been sending the rays of His love to draw us to Himself. The purpose is twofold. First, it respects service or fruit. "That ye may go." That word hints at parting, gives them a quasi-independent position, and yet shows the real union in separation. Wherever we go in obedience to His will, we carry His friendship. "That ye may bring forth fruit." This recalls the parable. Both ideas of keeping commandments and bringing forth fruit are needed to set forth the whole truth of Christian service. It is more than effortless growth or than painful effort. There must be first unity of life with Jesus, and then toil. Both are essential. "That your fruit should remain." Nothing corrupts faster than fruit. One sort only is incorruptible. The only activity that outlasts time and the world is that of those whose deeds are begun, continued, and ended in Him.

The other half of the issues of friendship with Jesus is the satisfaction of our desires, stated in substantially the same terms as we have already considered. To "ask in Christ's name" is more than merely to put that name as a kind of charm at the end of our prayers. It is to ask as—in some sense—His representatives, filled with His spirit, as well as in reliance on His sacrifice and intercession. Such prayers will not be self-willed, but in accordance with the will of Christ, and therefore of God; and therefore they will be answered. If we make Christ's desires ours, and our desires Christ's, they will be satisfied.

LESSON XVIII

The Spirit Convicting the World and Guiding the Church

St. John xvi. 1-15

1. "These things have I spoken unto you, that ye should not be offended.
2. They shall put you out of the synagogues: yea, the time cometh, that whosoever killeth you will think that he doeth God service.
3. And these things will they do unto you, because they have not known the Father, nor Me.
4. But these things have I told you, that when the time shall come, ye may remember that I told you of them. And these things I said not unto you at the beginning, because I was with you.
5. But now I go My way to Him that sent Me; and none of you asketh Me, Whither goest Thou?
6. But because I have said these things unto you, sorrow hath filled your heart.
7. Nevertheless I tell you the truth; It is expedient for you that I go away: for if I go not away, the Comforter will not come unto you; but if I depart, I will send Him unto you.
8. And when He is come, He will reprove the world of sin, and of righteousness, and of judgment:
9. Of sin, because they believe not on Me;
10. Of righteousness, because I go to My Father, and ye see Me no more.
11. Of judgment, because the prince of this world is judged.
12. I have yet many things to say unto you, but ye cannot bear them now.
13. Howbeit when He, the Spirit of truth, is come, He will guide you into all truth: for He shall not speak of Himself; but whatsoever He shall hear, that shall He speak: and He will show you things to come.
14. He shall glorify Me: for He shall receive of Mine, and shall show it unto you.
15. All things that the Father hath are Mine: therefore said I, that He shall take of Mine, and shall show it unto you."

THE unbroken flow of thought and many subtle links of connection in this wonderful discourse baffle attempts to group its deep teachings in any rigid sequence. But we can trace in this lesson three main ideas, which may assist us in grasping its significance if we keep in view.

I. Verses 1-6 are a kind of landing-place or pause in the discourse, mainly looking back on the previous utterances, and contemplating the reasons for speech now and silence before. First, in verses 1-4 the reasons for speech now are given in a double form,—"that ye should not be made to stumble" (ver. 1), and "that when the time shall come, ye may remember that I told you of them" (ver. 4). These two views of the reasons for speech are separated by a reiteration, in more emphatic form, of the dark prospect of persecution.

In the previous chapter the disciples were taught to expect the hatred of "the world," but here that world is formally identified with the apostate Jewish Church. "The synagogue" is "the world." The organised body calling itself God's Church may become the most rampant enemy of Christ's people and the fullest embodiment of all that makes "the world." Such a body will do the cruellest things religiously, and offer up Christ's servants as sacrifices to God. That is partly aggravation and partly alleviation of the sin. A Church which has become "world" will persecute as a duty; and the reason is that, although it may be rigidly orthodox and versed in theology, it "does not know" either God or Christ. It does not know the former because it will not know the latter.

The first reason which Jesus gives for present speech is that the disciples might be kept from stumbling when the forewarned evils burst on them. The stumbling-block for them in finding themselves at odds with the synagogue as to the claims of Jesus is of such magnitude as we can scarcely realise. But forewarned is forearmed, and that is as true about our difficulties as about theirs. If we try to follow Christ, we shall often have to stand in such a very small minority, and have against us such a mass who take such a different view of duty, that we shall be tempted to distrust our own consciences and to yield. We shall be heartened to stand firm if we remember Christ's warnings. So is it also in regard to other sorrows and trials. We have fair and full warning of them. Jesus does not enlist recruits by rose-tinted pictures of delights and concealment of trials in His service, but lets us understand from the beginning that we must make up our minds to antagonisms that we might otherwise escape, and "enter the kingdom through much tribulation." Sorrow anticipated is half overcome. Sorrow foretold gives confidence in our Guide. He has told us this, and He is right. If there were anything worse, He would have told us, and He will be right, too, in His predictions of good. He foretold Marah and its bitter waters; shall we not trust Him when He foretells Elim and its wells and palms?

"When their hour is come," says Jesus. "Their hour" is their appointed time. Who appointed it? He did, and therefore their punctual arrival up to time shows that they come in obedience to Him. Further, we have His reasons for past silence,—"Not unto you from the beginning, for I was with you." There had been passing hints before, but no such detailed exhibition, and that because He was still with them. That expresses superb confidence in His power to shield them. No harm can come as long as He is with them.

For us, too, sorrows though foretold in general terms, are largely hidden till near. There needs an adaptation of ear to word, which only experience gives. Great tracts of Scripture lie dark to us till life explains them, and then they come on us with the force of a new revelation, like the messages which of old were sent by a roll of parchment coiled upon a baton and then written upon, and were unintelligible unless the receiver had a corresponding roller to wrap them round. Thank God for the loving reticence as well as for the loving frankness of His forewarnings of sorrow!

One more thought lies here; namely, that the imperfect apprehension of Christ's words leads to sorrow instead of joy (vers. 5, 6). He had been telling them that He was "going," and all that they thought was "Going! then what is to become of *us*?" If there had been more love to Him, and they had said "Going! then what is to become of *Him*?" sorrow would not have filled their hearts, but joy would have flooded out sorrow, because He went to Him that sent Him, and therefore went with His work done. The steadfast contemplation of the ascended Christ is a sovereign antidote against solitude, the victory over a hostile world, the cure for every sorrow.

II. Verses 7-11 set forth one aspect of that gift of the Spirit, which has already been promised in these parting words; namely, its operation on "the world" through the disciples. Think of these eleven poor men and their peasant Leader at that moment. They were neither very wise nor strong, and outside that upper room there was scarcely a creature who had the least belief in either Him or them. They had everything against them, and, most of all, their own hearts, while they had nothing for them but their Master's promises. They were desolate at the thought of His going. And now He bids them think of that going away as pure gain for them, and explains that staggering statement by the assurance of the coming of the Spirit.

Paul said, "To abide in the flesh is more needful for you." Jesus said, "It is expedient for you that I go away." Why this difference? Because of the essential difference of the relation of the two to those whom they left. Paul's work ended when he went; Jesus' continued after He went. He is nearer us when He has left us, and works more mightily for us after departure. Death drops an iron gate between the dead and the living, through which no helping hand can be stretched, but Christ's influence flows unchecked through the grated door. Who is He of whom this is true, and what sort of work is that which is continued and perfected after death?

Here again we meet the declaration that the Spirit's coming is inseparably connected with Christ's departure. The complete work of Christ was the necessary preliminary, and, in some sense, the procuring cause of that gift; and since the Word is the Spirit's instrument, the revelation must be complete before the application of it can begin in its full energy. Christ must be at the right hand of God before He can bestow that Spirit, ascending on high that He may receive for, and give the gift to, spirits fitted to receive it by faith in His completed work.

It is by being "sent unto you" that the Spirit is to "convict the world"; that is to say, the subject in hand here is the conviction wrought by the Spirit using Christian men as its organs. Note the process of "conviction," which is no mere demonstration of truth. Certain facts are borne in upon understanding and conscience, and along with these, the conviction of error and fault in relation to them. "He shall convict the world in respect of sin." That is the first step towards the world's ceasing to be "world." Apart from the conviction of sin which is characteristic of the gospel, men have wholly inadequate notions of what it is, its inwardness, universality, and gravity as affecting man's whole being and relation to God. Every blunder and heresy that leads men away from the true conception of Christ and His work may be traced to defective notions or realisation of the fact of sin.

After the conviction of sin comes the dawning of the sunrise of righteousness. Obviously, "the world" is the subject throughout these verses. It is to be convinced, and it must be its sin and its righteousness and its judgment which are in view. There is but one way by which a conviction of righteousness as mine can follow one of sin as mine; namely, by the sight of a righteousness given from above, to sweep away my sin, and make me righteous as Christ is. That conviction will not be ours unless the other has gone before. The one conviction without the other is misery; the second without the first is irrelevant, as medicine to a man that thinks himself well.

Finally comes the conviction of "judgment." If there are in the world sin and righteousness, and the two collide, what then? Which will go down? Righteousness will triumph, and there will be "judgment," which will destroy the sin. There is a continual judgment going on now, and there is a future one beyond the grave. That is a terrible, but also a blessed, thought; terrible if I do not make that righteousness mine, blessed if I do, since it assures me that in the one case I must perish with the sin to which I cling, and in the other that I shall be separated from all my evil, and filled with perfect righteousness.

This threefold conviction which the Spirit in believers will work in the world rests on three facts: one of experience, one of history, and one of revelation,—all three having reference to Jesus and His relation to men. These are, the world's unbelief, Christ's ascension, and the judgment of the Prince of the world. Unbelief in Jesus is the climax and strongest proof of sin. Strange words! Here is a Man who dares to say that, full as the world is of hideous crimes, a mere negative and inward thing, namely, men's rejection of Him, is worst of all. What does the rejection of Christ betray the rejecter to be? He turns away from the loftiest, tenderest revelation of God's love, seeing nothing there to desire. Surely that augurs criminal blindness. He rejects the blessings of forgiveness, cleansing, and purity, and of a heaven which is the perfection of these. Surely that augurs earthly-mindedness gross and ignoble. The essence of sin is living to self. Belief in Christ is the surrender of self. So unbelief is a "typical" sin in its "purest" form. The mother-tincture is there concentrated which, variously coloured and perfumed, makes the evil of all sins.

There is a fact of history as the ground of the conviction of righteousness. He "goes to the Father and we see Him no more." He speaks as if the process had begun. His death, resurrection, and ascension are its stages. The apostles' great argument to convince the world of righteousness was to be the ascended Christ. With the supernatural fact of His ascension and abode with the Father stands or falls His power of giving us His own righteousness. If He cannot give me that, what does His having had it matter to me? Nothing. But if He is above to bestow upon us the law of the Spirit of Life in Him, which will make us free from the law of sin, then we may cherish hope that we too shall be made like Him. If He has gone to the Father, His righteousness may be the world's; if He has not, it is useless to any but Himself.

A fact made known only by revelation, the judgment of the Prince of the world, is the ground of the final conviction. The world has a Prince. However ludicrous vulgar superstitions may have made the notion, there is nothing ridiculous, nor anything which we have the right to call incredible, in Christ's solemn declaration that the kingdom of darkness has a King. The Cross was the judgment of that Prince, as is frequently taught in Scripture. Then the power of evil was broken in its centre. The serpent's head has been bruised, though still it writhes and swings " the scaly horror of its folded tail." But the strong man is bound, and his house is being spoiled. The judgment of the Prince prophesies the judgment of the world. That thought ought to be a hope, but it often is a fear. Whether hope or fear, it is a fact as certain as the Cross in the past or the throne in the present. If we know our own sin, and Christ's righteousness as ours, we can rejoice in the hope of the final judgment, and have boldness before Him when it comes.

III. I can but glance at the final portion of the lesson, in which the aspect of the Spirit's work as the Guide into all truth for believing souls is presented (vers. 12-15). Note the avowed incompleteness of Christ's own teaching (ver. 12). How does this representation agree with the other that He had made known "all things whatsoever He had heard of the Father"? There is a difference between bud and flower, principles and their development. He did give the fundamental, seminal principles, but not their unfolding, their consequences, or their mutual relations. As to these, there was much to be said which the disciples were not able to "carry."

People tell us, "Your modern theology isn't in the Gospels; we stick by Jesus, not by Paul." I do not admit that the silence of Jesus about His sacrificial death and the atoning power of it is so absolute; but I do admit that He says little about it. What then? That reticence is exactly what He told us we should find in His words. The Cross had to be endured before it could be explained. Jesus came to be the sacrifice, not to speak about it. Those who say that they take His words as the only source of their Christianity are flying in the face of His words in saying so; for He proclaimed their incompleteness, and referred us for fuller knowledge to a subsequent teacher.

Next we have declared the completeness of the truth into which the Spirit leads. Mark the personality of the Spirit,—"He," not "it." Note His designation as "the Spirit of truth," which is His characteristic and weapon. Note His office—"shall guide," as with a loving hand put out to lead, so suggesting the graciousness, gentleness, and gradualness of the teaching. Note the width of the promise, "all truth." That is not a promise of omniscience, but the assurance of gradual and growing acquaintance with the spiritual truth revealed in Jesus. Not to-day, nor to-morrow, will it all be known, but step by step we shall be led.

"He shall not speak of Himself; but whatsoever He shall hear, that shall He speak." The Spirit stands to Jesus as Jesus stands to the Father. Where does the Spirit "hear"? In the depths of Deity. And especially "things to come" would be made known—the evolving glory of the kingdom, and "all the wonder that should be"—in the new order which Christ should establish. It might appear as if two independent sources of illumination were set forth. Therefore in the last verses of the lesson we see the union of the two beams. "He shall glorify Me." Think of a man saying that! So fair is Christ that to make Him known is to make Him glorious. "He shall take of Mine." All the Spirit brings is Christ's; His office is not to give new revelation, but to interpret that given. He guides into "the truth," which Jesus declared Himself to be.

"All things that the Father hath are Mine: therefore said I, that He shall take of Mine, and shall show it unto you." What awful words! A Divine teaching Spirit can only teach concerning God, and Christ here explains the preceding words, in which, if He were but human, He had given that Spirit an unworthy office, by the solemn, articulate claim that whatever is God's is His, and whatever is His is God's. He puts out an unpresumptuous hand and lays hold on all the constellated glories of the Divine nature, saying, "They are Mine"; and the Father admits the claim, and answers, "Son, Thou art ever with Me, and all that I have is Thine." Let us add our "Amen," and trust our all to Him who makes us possessors of all that is His, that so we may be "filled with all the fulness of God."

LESSON XIX

The Intercessor

St. John xvii. 1-19

1. "These words spake Jesus, and lifted up His eyes to heaven, and said, Father, the hour is come; glorify Thy Son, that Thy Son also may glorify Thee:
2. As Thou hast given Him power over all flesh, that He should give eternal life to as many as Thou hast given Him.
3. And this is life eternal, that they might know Thee the only true God, and Jesus Christ, whom Thou hast sent.
4. I have glorified Thee on the earth: I have finished the work which Thou gavest Me to do.
5. And now, O Father, glorify Thou Me with Thine own self with the glory which I had with Thee before the world was.
6. I have manifested Thy name unto the men which Thou gavest Me out of the world: Thine they were, and Thou gavest them Me; and they have kept Thy word.
7. Now they have known that all things whatsoever Thou hast given Me are of Thee.
8. For I have given unto them the words which Thou gavest Me; and they have received them, and have known surely that I came out from Thee, and they have believed that Thou didst send Me.
9. I pray for them: I pray not for the world, but for them which Thou hast given Me; for they are Thine.
10. And all Mine are Thine, and Thine are Mine; and I am glorified in them.
11. And now I am no more in the world, but these are in the world, and I come to Thee. Holy Father, keep through Thine own name those whom Thou hast given Me, that they may be one, as we are.
12. While I was with them in the world, I kept them in Thy name: those that Thou gavest Me I have kept, and none of them is lost, but the son of perdition; that the Scripture might be fulfilled.
13. And now come I to Thee; and these things I speak in the world, that they might have My joy fulfilled in themselves.
14. I have given them Thy word; and the world hath hated them, because they are

not of the world, even as I am not of the world.

15. I pray not that Thou shouldest take them out of the world, but that Thou shouldest keep them from the evil.

16. They are not of the world, even as I am not of the world.

17. Sanctify them through Thy truth: Thy word is truth.

18. As Thou hast sent Me into the world, even so have I also sent them into the world.

19. And for their sakes I sanctify Myself, that they also might be sanctified through the truth."

WE may well despair of doing justice, in a lesson, to the deep thoughts of this prayer, which volumes would not exhaust. Who is worthy to speak or to write about such sacred words? Perhaps we may best gain some glimpses of their great and holy sublimity by trying to gather their teaching round the centres of the three petitions,—"glorify" (vers. 1, 5), "keep" (ver. 11), and "sanctify" (ver. 17).

I. In verses 1-5 Jesus prays for Himself, that He may be restored to His pre-incarnate glory; but yet the prayer desires not so much that glory as affecting Himself, as His being fitted thereby for completing His work of manifesting the Father. There are three main points in these verses,—the petition, its purpose, and its grounds.

As to the first, the repetition of the request in verses 1 and 5 is significant, especially if we note that in the former the language is impersonal, "Thy Son," and continues so till verse 4, where "I" and "Me" appear. In verses 1-3, then, the prayer rests upon the ideal relations of Father and Son, realised in Jesus, while in verses 4 and 5 the personal element is emphatically presented. The two petitions are in their scope identical. The "glorifying" in the former is more fully explained in the latter as being that which He possessed in that ineffable fellowship with the Father, not merely before incarnation, but before creation. In His manhood He possessed and manifested the "glory as of the only begotten of the Father, full of grace and truth"; but that glory, lustrous though it was, was pale, and humiliation compared with the light inaccessible, which shone around the eternal Word in the bosom of the Father. Yet He who prayed was the same Person who had walked in that light before time was, and now in human flesh asked for what no mere manhood could bear. The first form of the petition implies that such a partaking in the uncreated glory of the Father is the natural prerogative of One who is "the Son," while the second implies that it is the appropriate recompense of the earthly life and character of the man Jesus.

The petition not only reveals the conscious Divinity of the Son, but also His willing acceptance of the cross; for the glorifying sought is that reached through death, resurrection, and ascension, and that introductory clause "the hour is come" points to the impending sufferings as the first step in the answer to the petition. The crucifixion is always thus treated in this Gospel, as being both the lowest humiliation and the "lifting up" of the Son; and here He is reaching out His hand, as it were, to draw His sufferings nearer. So willingly and desiringly did this Isaac climb the mount of sacrifice. Both elements of the great saying in the Epistle to the Hebrews are here: "For the joy that was set before Him [He] endured the cross."

The purpose of the petition is to be noted; namely, the Son's glorifying of the Father. No taint of selfishness corrupted His prayer. Not for Himself, but for men, did He desire His glory. He sought return to that serene and lofty seat, and the elevation of His weak manhood to the throne, not because He was wearied of earth or impatient of weakness, sorrows, or limitations, but that He might more fully manifest, from that glory, the Father's name. To make the Father known is to make the Father glorious; for He is all fair and lovely. That revelation of Divine perfection, majesty, and sweetness was the end of Christ's earthly life, and is the end of His heavenly Divine activity. He needs to reassume the prerogatives of which He needed to divest Himself, and both necessities are one. He had to lay aside His garments and assume the form of a servant that He might make God known; but, that revelation being complete, He must take His garments and sit down again, before He can go on to tell all the meaning of what He has "done unto us."

The ground of the petition is twofold. Verses 2 and 3 represent the glory sought for, as the completion of the Son's mission and task. Already He had been endowed with authority over all flesh, for the purpose of bestowing eternal life; and that eternal life stands in the knowledge of God, which is the same as the knowledge of Christ. The present gift to the Son and its purpose are thus precisely parallel with the further gift desired, and that is the necessary carrying out of this. The authority and office of the incarnate Christ demand the glory of and consequent further manifestation by the glorified Christ. The life which He comes to give is a life which flows from the revelation He makes of the Father, received, not as mere intellectual knowledge, but as loving acquaintance.

The second ground for the petition is in verse 4, the actual perfect fulfilment by the Son of that mission. What untroubled consciousness of sinless obedience and transparent shining through His life of the Father's likeness and will He must have had who could thus assert His complete realisation of that Father's revealing purpose, as the ground of His deserving and desiring participation in the Divine glory! Surely such words are either the acme of self-righteousness or the self-revealing speech of the Son of God.

II. With verse 6 we pass to the more immediate reference to the disciples, and the context from thence to verse 15 may be regarded as all clustered round the second petition, "keep" (ver. 11). That central request is preceded and followed by consideration of the disciples' relation to Christ and to the world, which may be regarded as its grounds. The whole context preceding the petition may be summed up in two grounds for the prayer,—the former set forth at length, and the latter summarily; the one being the genuine, though incomplete, discipleship of the men for whom Christ prays (vers. 6-10), and the latter their desolate condition without Jesus (ver. 11).

It is beautiful to see how our Lord here credits the disciples with genuine grasp, both in heart and head, of His teaching. He had shortly before had to say, "Have I been so long time with you, and yet hast thou not known Me?" and soon "they all forsook Him and fled." But beneath misconception and inadequate apprehension there lived faith and love; and He saw the full corn in the ear, when only the green blade was visible, pushing itself above the surface. We may take comfort from this generous estimate of imperfect disciples. If He did not tend, instead of quenching, dimly burning wicks, where would He have "lights in the world"?

Verse 6 lays down the beginning of discipleship as threefold: Christ's act in revealing; the Father's, in giving men to Jesus; and men's, in keeping the Father's word. "Thy word" is the whole revelation by Christ, which is, as this Gospel so often repeats, not His own, but the Father's. These three facts underlying discipleship are pleas for the petition to follow; for unless the feeble disciples are "kept" in the name, as in a fortress, Christ's work of revelation is neutralised, the Father's gift to Him made of none effect, and the incipient disciples will not "keep" His word. The plea is, in effect, "Forsake not the works of Thine own hands"; and, like all Christ's prayers, it has a promise in its depths, since God does not begin what He will not finish; and it has a warning, too, that we cannot keep ourselves unless a stronger hand keeps us.

Verses 7 and 8 carry on the portraiture of discipleship, and thence draw fresh pleas. The blessed result of accepting Christ's revelation is a knowledge, built on happy experience, and, like the acquaintance of heart with heart, issuing in the firm conviction that Christ's words and deeds are from God. Why does He say, "All things whatsoever Thou hast given," instead of simply "that I have" or "declare"? Probably it is the natural expression of His consciousness, the lowly utterance of His obedience, claiming nothing as His own, and yet claiming all, while the subsequent clause "are of Thee" expresses the disciples' conviction. In like fashion our Lord, in verse 8, declares that His words, in their manifoldness (contrast ver. 6, "Thy word"), were all received by Him from the Father, and accepted by the disciples, with the result that they came, as before, to "know" by inward acquaintance with Him as a person, and so to have the Divinity of His person certified by experience, and further came to "believe" that God had sent Him, which was a conviction arrived at by faith. So knowledge, which is personal experience and acquaintance, and faith, which rises to the heights of the Father's purpose, come from the humble acceptance of the Christ declaring the Father's name. First faith, then knowledge, and then a fuller faith built on it, and that faith in its turn passing into knowledge (ver. 25),—these are the blessings belonging to the growth of true discipleship, and are discerned by the loving eye of Jesus in very imperfect followers.

In verse 9 Jesus assumes the great office of Intercessor. "I pray for them" is not so much prayer as His solemn presentation of Himself before the Father as the High Priest of His people. It marks an epoch in His work. The task of bringing God to man is substantially complete. That of bringing men by supplication to God is now to begin. It is the revelation of the permanent office of the departed Lord. Moses on the Mount holds up the rod, and Israel prevails (Exod. xvii. 9). The limitation of this prayer to the disciples applies only to the special occasion, and has no bearing on the sweep of His redeeming purpose or the desires of His all-pitying heart. The reasons for His intercession follow in verses 9-11 a. The disciples are the Father's, and continue so even when "given" to Christ, in accordance with the community of possession which oneness of nature and perfectness of love establish between the Father and the Son. God cannot but care for those who are His. The Son cannot but pray for those who are His. Their having recognised Him for what He was binds Him to pray for them. He is glorified in disciples, and if we show forth His character He will be our Advocate. The last reason for His prayer is the loneliness of the disciples and their exposure in the world without Him. His departure impelled Him to intercede, both as being a leaving them defenceless and as being an entrance into the heavenly state of communion with the Father.

In the petition itself (ver. 11), observe the invocation "Holy Father," with special reference to the prayer for preservation from the corruption of the world. God's holiness is the pledge that He will make us holy, since He is Father as well. Observe the substance of the request, that the disciples should be kept, as in a fortress, within the enclosing circle of the name which God has given to Jesus. The name is the manifestation of the Divine nature. It was given to Jesus, inasmuch as He, the Word, had from the beginning the office of revealing God; and that which was spoken of the angel of the covenant is true in highest reality of Jesus: "My name is in Him." "The name of the Lord is a strong tower: the righteous runneth into it and is safe."

Observe the issue of this keeping; namely, the unity of believers. The depths of that saying are beyond us, but we can at least see thus far,—that the true bond of unity is the name in which all who are one are kept; that the pattern of the true unity of believers is the ineffable union of Father and Son, which is oneness of will and nature, along with distinctness of persons; and that therefore this purpose goes far deeper than outward unity of organisation.

Then follow other pleas, which are principally drawn

from Christ's relation to the disciples, now ending; whereas the former ones were chiefly deduced from the disciples' relation to Him. He can no more do what He has done, and commits it to the Father. Happy we if we can leave our unfinished tasks to be taken up by God, and trust those whom we leave undefended to be shielded by Him! "I kept" is, in the Greek, expressive of continuous, repeated action, while "I guarded" gives the single issue of the many acts of keeping. Jesus keeps His disciples now as He did then, by sedulous, patient, reiterated acts, so that they are safe from evil. But note where He kept,—"in Thy name." That is our place of safety, a sure defence and inexpugnable fortress. One, indeed, was lost; but that was not any slur on Christ's keeping, but resulted from his own evil nature, as being "a son of loss" (if we may so preserve the affinity of words in the Greek), and from the Divine decree from of old. Sharply defined and closely united are the two apparent contradictories of man's free choice of destruction and God's foreknowledge. Christ saw them in harmony, and we shall do so one day.

Then the flow of the prayer recurs to former thoughts. Going away so soon He yearned to leave them sharers of His own emotions in the prospect of His departure to the Father, and therefore He had admitted them (and us) to hear this sacred outpouring of His desires. If we laid to heart the blessed revelations of this disclosure or Christ's heart, and followed Him with faithful gaze as He ascends to the Father, and realised our share in that triumph, our empty vessels would be filled by some of that same joy which was His. Earthly joy can never be full; Christian joy should never be anything less than full.

Then follows a final glance at the disciples' relation to the world, to which they are alien because they are of kindred to Him. This is the ground for the repetition of the prayer "keep," with the difference that formerly it was "keep *in* Thy name," and now it is "*from* the evil." It is good to gaze first on our defence, the munitions of rocks where we lie safely, and then we can venture to face the thought of " the evil " from which that keeps us, whether it be personal or abstract.

III. Verses 16-19 give the final petition for the immediate circle of disciples, with its grounds. The position of alienation from the world, in which the disciples stand by reason of their assimilation to Jesus, is repeated here. It was the reason for the former prayer, "keep"; it is the reason for the new petition, "sanctify." Keeping comes first, and then sanctifying, or consecration. Security from evil is given that we may be wholly devoted to the service of God. The evil in the world is the great hindrance to that. The likeness to Jesus is the great ground of hope that we shall be truly consecrated. We are kept " in the name "; we are consecrated " in the truth," which is the revelation made by Jesus, and in a very deep sense is Himself. That truth is, as it were, the element in which the believer lives, and by abiding in which His real consecration is possible.

Christ's prayer for us should be our aim and deepest desire for ourselves, and His declaration of the condition of its fulfilment should prescribe our firm adhesion to, and constant abiding in, the truth as revealed and embodied in Him, as the only means by which we can attain the consecration which is at once, as the closing verses of the lesson tell us, the means by which we may fulfil the purpose for which we are sent into the world, and the path on which we reach complete assimilation to His perfect self-surrender. All Christians are sent into the world by Jesus, as Jesus was sent by the Father. We have the charge to glorify Him. We have the presence of the Sender with us, the sent. We are inspired with His Spirit. We cannot do His work without that entire consecration which shall copy His devotion to the Father and eager swiftness to do His will. How can such ennobling and exalted consecration be ours? There is but one way. He has "consecrated Himself," and by union with Him, through faith, our selfishness may be subdued, and the Spirit of Christ may dwell in our hearts, to make us "living sacrifices, consecrated and acceptable to God." Then shall we be "truly consecrated," and then alone, when we can say, "I live; yet not I, but Christ liveth in me." That is the end of Christ's consecration of Himself,—the prayer which He prayed for His disciples,—and should be the aim which every disciple earnestly pursues.

LESSON XX

The Willing Prisoner

ST. JOHN xviii. 1-13

1. "When Jesus had spoken these words, He went forth with His disciples over the brook Cedron, where was a garden, into the which He entered, and His disciples.

2. And Judas also, which betrayed Him, knew the place: for Jesus ofttimes resorted thither with His disciples.

3. Judas then, having received a band of men and officers from the chief priests and Pharisees, cometh thither with lanterns and torches and weapons.

4. Jesus therefore, knowing all things that should come upon Him, went forth, and said unto them, Whom seek ye?

5. They answered Him, Jesus of Nazareth. Jesus saith unto them, I am He. And Judas also, which betrayed Him, stood with them.

6. As soon then as He had said unto them, I am He, they went backward, and fell to the ground.

7. Then asked He them again, Whom seek ye? And they said, Jesus of Nazareth.

8. Jesus answered, I have told you that I am He: if therefore ye seek Me, let these go their way:

9. That the saying might be fulfilled, which He spake, Of them which Thou gavest Me have I lost none.

10. Then Simon Peter having a sword drew it, and smote the high priest's servant, and cut off his right ear. The servant's name was Malchus.

11. Then said Jesus unto Peter, Put up thy sword into the sheath: the cup which My Father hath given Me, shall I not drink it?

12. Then the band and the captain and officers of the Jews took Jesus, and bound Him,

13. And led Him away to Annas first; for he was father in law to Caiaphas, which was the high priest that same year."

JOHN'S omissions and additions in this section are equally significant. He has no mention of the agony in Gethsemane, and he alone records the remarkable incident of the panic which shook the soldiers. His narrative is most naturally taken here, as everywhere, as a supplement to the Synoptics, for the special purpose of bringing out the facts which showed Jesus to be "the Son of God." This is his own account of his design, and is well illustrated in this lesson.

I. We have the two so different companies converging on the one spot. It is only John who mentions the passage of the Kidron, the generally dry torrent-bed between the temple mount and Olivet, which had seen the crossing of another king of Israel, a fugitive from a traitor son (2 Sam. xv. 23). John alone tells us that the place was "a garden." Gethsemane witnessed victory; Eden saw defeat. The place seems to have been chosen not only for quiet and seclusion, but because it was His habitual resort, and may even have been His usual open-air sleeping-place (John viii. 1). The reference to Judas' knowledge of the place implies that that knowledge was one reason for its selection. The motive for secrecy was past since His "desire to eat this passover with you" was fulfilled, and now Jesus seems to smooth the path for His captors.

On the one hand, then, we see the little band coming from the city in deep silence, and passing into the olive-garden, where the tremulous shadows of the leaves somewhat obscured the paschal moon; and, on the other, we see the armed soldiers of the Roman garrison and the temple police, headed by Judas, and carrying useless swords which had no power against Jesus, and superfluous "lanterns and torches," which were absurd in that clear moonlight. The contrast of the two groups is striking as they pass through the silent midnight to meet beneath the olives. One starts from heaven, the other from hell, and they touch there. Infinite love and the mystery of Divine endurance for man stream from the one, like the encircling moonbeams; diabolic hate and treachery flame in the other, like the smoky torches with which they affronted the moon. How many opposing paths met in that meeting! John has no record of the solemn scene in the depths of the garden. He takes the readers' knowledge of it for granted; but he fixes our attention on these two groups, and wishes us to feel the impressiveness of the contrast, as well as the voluntary surrender of Jesus to His captors, implied in His choice of the place.

II. John's special contributions to the narrative of our Lord's capture are the momentary flash of glory which struck awe into the band, and the care of Jesus for His disciples' safety even in that supreme moment. What calm majesty there is in His coming forth from the garden to meet the approaching crowd, and how His willing surrender, not so much to the violence of men as to the purpose of the Father, is expressed in that explanation of the consciousness which impelled Him, as a similar consciousness had led Him to gird Himself with the towel! Probably Judas' kiss was given at this first meeting with the band; but, as would be likely in the uncertain light (made more uncertain by the torches) and confusion, it was unnoticed by most, and the traitor slunk back among the others, as he appears in verse five.

The quiet question "Whom seek ye?" fell on the ears of the foremost ranks of the captors. Did it remind John of the other, so like and yet so unlike it, "What seek ye?" which had drawn him to Jesus at first? Its purpose was apparently to protect the disciples, and perhaps to appeal to the conscience of some among the tools of the priests. If men would put their sinful purposes into plain words, they would sometimes shrink from executing them. But here the answer came from many lips, and was not without a shade of contempt for their prey, "Jesus the Nazarene." They did not suppose that their questioner was their prisoner; and when the tranquil voice said "I am He," they recoiled, and some of them "fell to the ground," perhaps thrown down by the falling back of the front ranks.

We need not ask if this was a miracle. However produced, a strange awe and terror smote the rude soldiers. His calm dignity impressed them, as that of virgin martyrs and grey-headed confessors has often done. But that will not explain the fact, which seems most worthily attributed to a momentary shining forth of Christ's indwelling divinity, somewhat like that which shone through His corporeal frame at the transfiguration. It may not have been the work of His will at all, but the elevation of spirit attendant on the solemn scene in Gethsemane may have transfigured for a moment His lowly manhood, and let some beams of His glory through. But however that may be, we can scarcely fail to see here a revelation of His majesty, which is all the more eloquent as coming at the hour of deepest humiliation.

We have frequently had occasion to note how John delights to bring into juxtaposition instances of both, as indeed do all the evangelists. The interweaving of lowliness and glory makes the very *differentia* of the character portrayed by them all. He is a weak infant, but angels hover round the manger, and a star leads worshippers to it. He bows His head to John's baptism, but heaven opens and the dove descends. He falls asleep in the boat, but wakes to still the storm with a word. He weeps by a grave, but He raises its tenant. He all but faints in His agony in the garden, but angels strengthen Him. The same union of opposites is in this incident. He is to be led, bound by rude hands, before an unjust judge. But as He passes into their power, one flash of brightness "above that of the noonday sun" tells of the hidden glory. "What will He do when He shall come as judge, if He did this when giving Himself up as a prisoner?" (Augustine.)

The moment was propitious for escape, if He had chosen, as the soldiers lay huddled together in terror. Why did He not pass through the midst of them, and go His way? It would have been perfectly easy. But, instead, He stands still and repeats the question. Verse seven literally reads "*Therefore* He asked them again," which suggests that the second putting of the question was meant to stimulate the soldiers to their office. Thus here again, even if that interpretation of the "Therefore" be not sustained, we have a distinct instance, in the facts themselves, of Christ's voluntary surrender to the fate which He could easily have avoided. Not only in the great resolve to enter into our human limitations, but step by step, through all His earthly life, His steadfast will travelled towards the Cross; and the voluntariness of His death is most strongly marked in the events of that last journey to Jerusalem, and especially of the final days there. The studied publicity—and we had almost said offensiveness to the rulers—of His last entrance and utterances; the withdrawal till the passover; the precautions against interruption at the Last Supper; the resort to the usual place, Gethsemane; and this refusal to avail Himself of the means of safety open to Him at this last moment,—are all of one piece, and present Him, not as the passive Victim of men's hate, but as the voluntary Sacrifice, who chooses time and place for the consummate act of His love and of our redemption. "No man taketh it from Me, but I lay it down of Myself." His death was His act. He died because He chose, and He chose because He would obey the Father and loved the world. This Sacrifice was not bound to the altar, but laid Himself willingly there; or, if bound at all, it was with "cords of love."

The last word to the captors explains the motive for the previous repeated question as being the shielding of the disciples, by the clear definition of the limitation of the arrest to Himself. The disciples were innocent, and they were unfit for such a trial. One day many of them would have to die for Him, but not yet. So, even at that hour of peril for Himself, all His care is for His humble friends, and He was ready to yield Himself to bonds and death to secure their liberty. "Let these go their way" gives the sheep permission to scatter, now that the Shepherd is taken. John sees in this a fulfilment, on a small scale, of the great words which he quotes from the intercessory prayer; not that he thought that such a trivial and transient matter exhausted their meaning, but he sees in it, as in a tiny mirror, the reflection of the much mightier, eternal safe-keeping of all Christ's servants. A dewdrop is rounded by the same law which shapes planets into spheres. The greatest may be shown in the smallest.

This incident is as a parable. It shows Christ's self-forgetting care. In it He gives Himself up as a prisoner, that His servants may go free. To all our foes He says, Take Me, and let these go. Guilt, sorrow, pains and ills, death and hell, are thus addressed, or rather commanded, by Him. His speech to them is, like that to His captors, authoritative, and liker the orders of a prince than the entreaty of a prisoner. Jesus has met our enemies like a mother who gives herself to the wolves that her children may escape. The transcendent sacrifice of His death is mirrored, in its principle and effects, in these wondrous words, "If ye seek Me, let these go their way."

III. The rash and futile attempt at resistance follows, in strong contrast to the unused power of overcoming by Divine might, which Jesus willed to keep latent. He would not use the effectual defence which He possessed; but Peter, who with the others had by this time joined the company outside the enclosure, produces some sword which he had got hold of, and strikes at random. Half asleep, and dazzled by the uncertain light, and agitated, and probably more used to haul nets than handle swords, he happily missed the head, and took only an ear. An eyewitness is manifest in the specification of "the right ear."

It is right and easy to blame the rashness of Peter, but let him have the credit of brave devotion. It is easy to see that one sword flourished would only provoke twenty to leap from their scabbards, and bring on a hopeless struggle. But how many of us would have been courageous enough to have done what he did? Prudence is a very valuable virtue, but courage set on fire by love is better, and its condemnation, if it be sometimes rash, should be very lenient. John knew, and, now that so many years had passed, could venture to tell, the names of both actors in what had so nearly been a tragedy, which names the other evangelists either did not know, or thought it better to suppress.

Our Lord's command to sheathe his useless weapon is given in a form which implies the prayer in Gethsemane, which John does not record. He had asked that the cup should pass from Him, and the answer was the full acquiescence of His will in the Father's will that He should drink it. The cup was felt to be given, and that was better than that it should have been taken away. The best answer to our prayers is the submission of our wills and the recognition of the Father's hand as commending the chalice to our lips. The cup may remain, but its bitterness is taken away when we know it to be the "cup which our Father hath given us."

IV. The actual capture is briefly described. The soldiers of the Roman garrison and their officer are significantly named before the Jewish officials. Evidently the arrest was beyond the power of the priests without the help of Pilate, and also the co-operation of Gentile and Jew, which runs through the whole story of the passion, and points so deep truths, is meant to be noted from the beginning.

John alone records the appearance before Annas, and his remark that Jesus was led to his house "first" seems to imply that he wishes to supplement the other accounts, which tell only of Christ's appearance before Caiaphas. The name of the judge was sufficient to stamp the character of shameless injustice on the whole procedure. Annas had himself been high priest, and several of his sons, as well as his son-in-law Caiaphas, held the office in succession during his lifetime, in flagrant violation of the law for the high-priesthood. Such worldly intriguers, who prostituted their office for personal ends, were the judges before whom Jesus, the reality of which their desecrated office was the shadow, stood as a criminal. The irony of providence could no further go than that such a man as Annas or as Caiaphas should hold that position at such a time. And this it is which John would point out by his remark that Caiaphas, of all men in the world, should have been "high priest *that* year," the unworthy holder of the office which gave such a man power of life and death over Jesus. Caiaphas on the bench, and Jesus at the bar! What could the end of that be?

LESSON XXI

The Reluctant Judge, the Resolved Accusers, and the Patient Christ

ST. JOHN xix. 1-16

1. "Then Pilate therefore took Jesus, and scourged Him.

2. And the soldiers platted a crown of thorns, and put it on His head, and they put on Him a purple robe,

3. And said, Hail, King of the Jews! and they smote Him with their hands.

4. Pilate therefore went forth again, and saith unto them, Behold, I bring Him forth to you, that ye may know that I find no fault in Him.

5. Then came Jesus forth, wearing the crown of thorns, and the purple robe. And Pilate saith unto them, Behold the Man!

6. When the chief priests therefore and officers saw Him, they cried out, saying, Crucify Him, crucify Him. Pilate saith unto them, Take ye Him, and crucify Him: for I find no fault in Him.

7. The Jews answered him, We have a law, and by our law He ought to die, because He made Himself the Son of God.

8. When Pilate therefore heard that saying, he was the more afraid;

9. And went again into the judgment hall, and saith unto Jesus, Whence art Thou? But Jesus gave him no answer.

10. Then saith Pilate unto Him, Speakest Thou not unto me? knowest Thou not that I have power to crucify Thee, and have power to release Thee?

11. Jesus answered, Thou couldest have no power at all against Me, except it were given thee from above: therefore he that delivered Me unto thee hath the greater sin.

12. And from thenceforth Pilate sought to release Him: but the Jews cried out, saying, If thou let this Man go, thou art not Cæsar's friend: whosoever maketh himself a king speaketh against Cæsar.

13. When Pilate therefore heard that saying, he brought Jesus forth, and sat down in the judgment seat in a place that is called the Pavement, but in the Hebrew, Gabbatha.

14. And it was the preparation of the passover, and about

the sixth hour: and he saith unto the Jews, Behold your King!

15. But they cried out, Away with Him, away with Him, crucify Him. Pilate saith unto them, Shall I crucify your King? The chief priests answered, We have no king but Cæsar.

16. Then delivered he Him therefore unto them to be crucified. And they took Jesus, and led Him away."

THE struggle between the vacillation of Pilate and the fixed malignity of the rulers is the principal theme of this fragment of Christ's judicial trial. He Himself is passive and all but silent, speaking only one sentence of calm rebuke. The frequent changes of scene from within to without the prætorium indicate the steps in the struggle, and vividly reflect the irresolution of Pilate. These changes may help to mark the stages in the lesson.

I. The cruelties and indignities in verses 1-3 were inflicted within the "palace," to which Pilate, with his Prisoner, had returned after the rulers' vote for Barabbas. John makes that choice of the robber the reason for the scourging of Jesus. His thought seems to be that Pilate, having failed in his attempt to get rid of the whole difficulty by releasing Jesus, according to the "custom," ordered the scourging, in hope that the lighter punishment might satisfy the turbulent crowd, whom he wished to humour, while, if possible, saving their Victim. It was the expedient of a weak and cynical nature, and, like all weak attempts at compromise between right and wrong, only emboldened the hatred which it was meant to appease. If by clamour the rulers had succeeded in getting Pilate to scourge a Man whom he thought innocent, they might well hope to get him to crucify, if they clamoured loudly and long enough.

One attitude only befitted Pilate, since he did not in

the least believe that Jesus threatened the Roman supremacy; namely, to set Him at liberty, and let the disappointed rulers growl like wild beasts robbed of their prey. But he did not care enough about a single half-crazy Jewish peasant to risk his standing well with his awkward subjects, for the sake of righteousness. The one good which Rome could give to its vassal nations was inflexible justice and a sovereign law; but in Pilate's action there was not even the pretence of legality. Tricks and expedients run through it all, and never once does he say, This is the law, this is justice, and by it I stand or fall.

The cruel scourging which, in Roman hands, was a much more severe punishment than the Jewish "beating with rods," and often ended in death, was inflicted on the silent, unresisting Christ, not because His judge thought that it was deserved, but to please accusers whose charge he knew to be absurd. The underlings naturally followed their betters' example, and, after they had executed Pilate's orders to scourge, covered the bleeding wounds with some robe, perhaps ragged, but of the royal colour, and crushed the twisted wreath of thorn-branch down on the brows, to make fresh wounds there. The jest of crowning such a poor, helpless creature as Jesus seemed to them, was exactly on the level of such rude natures, and would be the more exquisite to them because it was double-barrelled, and insulted the nation as well as the "king." They came in a string, as the tense of the original word suggests, and offered their mock reverence. But that became tame after a little, and mockery passed into violence, as it always does in such natures. These rough legionaries were cruel and brutal, and they were unconscious witnesses to His kingship as founded on suffering; but they were innocent as compared with the polished gentleman who prostituted justice on the judgment-seat, and the learned Pharisees who were howling for blood outside.

II. In verses 4-8 the scene changes again to without the palace, and shows us Pilate trying another expedient, equally in vain. The hesitating governor has no chance with the resolute, rooted hate of the rulers. Jesus silently and unresistingly follows Pilate from the hall, still wearing the mockery of royal pomp. Pilate had calculated that the sight of Him in such guise, and bleeding from the lash, might turn hate into contempt, and perhaps give a touch of pity. "Behold the Man!" as he meant it, was as if he had said, "Is this poor, bruised, spiritless Sufferer worth hate or fear? Does He look like a king or a dangerous enemy?" Pilate for once drops the scoff of calling Him their king, and seeks to conciliate and move to pity. The profound meanings which later ages have delighted to find in his words, however warrantable, are no part of their design as spoken, and we gain a better lesson from the scene by keeping close to the thoughts of the actors. What a contrast between the vacillation of the governor, on the one hand, afraid to do right and reluctant to do wrong, and the dogged malignity of the rulers and their tools on the other, and the calm, meek endurance of the silent Christ, knowing all their thoughts, pitying all, and fixed in loving resolve, even firmer than the rulers' hate, to bear the utmost, that He might save a world!

Some pity may have stirred in the crowd, but the priests and their immediate dependants silenced it by the yell of fresh hate at the sight of the Prisoner. Note how John gives the very impression of the fierce, brief roar, like that of wild beasts for their prey, by his "Crucify, crucify," without addition of the person. Pilate lost patience at last, and angrily and half seriously gives permission to them to take the law into their own hands. He really means, "I will not be your tool, and, if my conviction of 'the Man's' innocence is to be of no account, you must punish Him; for I will not." How far he meant to abdicate authority, and how far he was launching sarcasms, it is difficult to say. Throughout he is sarcastic, and thereby indicates his weakness, indemnifying himself for being thwarted by sneers, which sit ill on authority.

But the offer, or sarcasm, whichever it was, missed fire, as the appeal to pity had done, and only led to the production of a new weapon. In their frantic determination to compass Jesus' death, the rulers hesitate at no degradation; and now they adduced the charge of blasphemy, and were ready to make a heathen the judge. To ask a 'Roman governor to execute their law on a religious offender, was to drag their national prerogative in the mud. But formal religionists, inflamed by religious animosity, are often the degraders of religion for the gratification of their hatred. They are poor preservers of the Church who call on the secular arm to execute their "laws." Rome went a long way in letting subject peoples keep their institutions; but it was too much to expect Pilate to be the hangman for these furious priests, on a charge scarcely intelligible to him.

What was Jesus doing while all this hell of wickedness and fury boiled round Him? Standing there, passive and dumb, "as a sheep before her shearers." Himself is the least conspicuous figure in the history of His own trial. In silent communion with the Father, in silent submission to His murderers, in silent pity for us, in silent contemplation of the joy that was set before Him, He waits on their will.

III. Once more the scene changes to the interior of the prætorium (vers. 9-11). The rulers' words stir a deepened awe in Pilate. He "was the more afraid." Then he had been already afraid. His wife's dream, the impression already produced by the person of Jesus, had touched him more deeply than probably he himself was aware of; and now this charge that Jesus had "made Himself the Son of God" shook him. What if this strange Man were in some sense a messenger of the gods? Had he been scourging one sent from them? Sceptical he probably was, and therefore superstitious; and half-forgotten and disbelieved stories of gods who had come down in the likeness of men would swim up in his memory. If this Man were such, His strange demeanour would be explained. Therefore he carried Jesus in again, and, not now as judge, sought to hear from His own lips His version of the alleged claim.

Why did not Jesus answer such a question? His silence was answer; but, besides that, Pilate had not received what Jesus had already declared to him as to His kingdom and His relation to "the truth" as he ought, and careless turning away from Christ's earlier words is righteously and necessarily punished by subsequent silence, if the same disposition remains. That it did remain Christ's silence is proof. Had there been any use in answering, Pilate would not have asked in vain.

If Jesus was silent, we may be sure that He who sees all hearts and responds to all true desires was so because He knew that it was best to say nothing. The question of His origin had nothing to do with Pilate's duty then, which turned, not on whence Jesus had come, but on what Pilate believed Him to have done, or not to have done. He who will not do the plain duty of the moment has little chance of an answer to his questions about such high matters.

The shallow character of the governor's awe and interest is clearly seen from the immediate change of tone to arrogant reminder of his absolute authority. "To me dost Thou not speak?" The pride of offended dignity peeps out there. He has forgotten that a moment since he half suspected that the Prisoner, whom he now seeks to terrify with the cross and to allure with deliverance, was perhaps come from some misty heaven. Was that a temper which would have received Christ's answer to his question?

But one thing he might be made to perceive, and therefore Jesus broke silence for the only time in this lesson, and almost the only time before Pilate. He reads the arrogant Roman the lesson which he and all his tribe in all lands and ages need,—that their power is derived from God, therefore in its foundation legitimate and in its exercise to be guided by His will and used for His purposes. It was God who had brought the Roman eagles, with their ravening beaks and strong claws, to the Holy City. Pilate was right in exercising jurisdiction over Jesus. Let him see that he exercised justice. And let him remember that the power which he boasted that he "had" was "given." The truth as to the source of power made the guilt of Caiaphas or of the rulers the greater, inasmuch as they had neglected the duties to which they had been appointed, and by handing over Jesus on a charge which they themselves should have searched out, had been guilty of "theocratic felony." This sudden flash of bold rebuke, reminding Pilate of his dependence, and charging him with "the lesser" but yet real "sin," went deeper than any answer to his question would have done, and spurred him to more earnest effort, as John points out. He "sought to release Him," as if formerly he had been rather simply unwilling to condemn than anxious to deliver.

IV. So the scene changes again to outside. He first went out alone, leaving Jesus within, and was met before he had time, as would appear, to speak, by the final irresistible weapon which the rulers had kept in reserve. An accusation of treason was only too certain to be listened to by the suspicious tyrant who was then emperor, especially if brought by the authorities of a subject nation. Many a provincial governor had had but a short shrift in such a case, and Pilate knew that he was a ruined man if these implacable zealots howling before him went to Tiberius with such a charge. So the die was cast. With rage in his heart, no doubt, and knowing that he was sacrificing innocent blood to save himself, he turned away from the victorious mob, apparently in silence, and brought Jesus out once more. He had no more words to say to his Prisoner. Nothing remained but the formal act of sentence, for which he seated himself, with a poor assumption of dignity, yet feeling all the while, no doubt, what a contemptible surrender he was making.

Judgment-seats and mosaic pavements do not go far to secure reverence for a judge who is no better than an assassin, killing an innocent man to secure his own ends. Pilate's sentence fell most heavily on himself. If "the judge is condemned when the guilty is acquitted," he is tenfold condemned when the innocent is sentenced.

Pilate returned to his sarcastic mood when he returned to his injustice, and found some satisfaction in his old jeer "your King." But the passion of hatred was too much in earnest to be turned or even affected by such poor scoffs, and the only answer was the renewed roar of the mob, which had murder in its tone. The repetition of the governor's taunt "Shall I crucify your King?" brought out the answer in which the rulers of the nation in their fury blindly flung away their prerogative. It is no accident that it was "the chief priests" who answered, "We have no king but Cæsar." Driven by hate, they deliberately disown their Messianic hope, and repudiate their national glory. They who will not have Christ have to bow to a tyrant. Rebellion against Him brings slavery.

LESSON XXII

"It is Finished"

St. John xix. 17-30

17. "And He bearing His cross went forth into a place called the place of a skull, which is called in the Hebrew Golgotha:

18. Where they crucified Him, and two other with Him, on either side one, and Jesus in the midst.

19. And Pilate wrote a title, and put it on the cross. And the writing was, JESUS OF NAZARETH THE KING OF THE JEWS.

20. This title then read many of the Jews: for the place where Jesus was crucified was nigh to the city: and it was written in Hebrew, and Greek, and Latin.

21. Then said the chief priests of the Jews to Pilate, Write not, The King of the Jews; but that He said, I am King of the Jews.

22. Pilate answered, What I have written I have written.

23. Then the soldiers, when they had crucified Jesus, took His garments, and made four parts, to every soldier a part; and also His coat: now the coat was without seam, woven from the top throughout.

24. They said therefore among themselves, Let us not rend it, but cast lots for it, whose it shall be: that the Scripture might be fulfilled, which saith, They parted My raiment among them, and for My vesture they did cast lots. These things therefore the soldiers did.

25. Now there stood by the cross of Jesus His mother, and His mother's sister, Mary the wife of Cleophas, and Mary Magdalene.

26. When Jesus therefore saw His mother, and the disciple standing by, whom He loved, He saith unto His mother, Woman, behold thy son!

26. Then saith He to the disciple, Behold thy mother! And from that hour that disciple took her unto his own home.

28. After this, Jesus knowing that all things were now accomplished, that the Scripture might be fulfilled, saith, I thirst.

29. Now there was set a vessel full of vinegar: and they filled a spunge with vinegar, and put it upon hyssop, and put it to His mouth.

30. When Jesus therefore had received the vinegar, He said, It is finished: and He bowed His head, and gave up the ghost."

THE supplementary character of John's account of the crucifixion is shown by both its omissions and additions, as compared with the other Gospels. These deserve careful examination. So far as any purpose beyond that of contributing incidents to complete the narratives can be discerned, we cannot but feel that the impression from the whole account is that of the calm majesty of voluntary suffering, in filial obedience fulfilling the will of the Father and the word of prophecy. Such an impression corresponds entirely to the point of view of John's Gospel, which is none the less trustworthy as a record of facts because the facts are chosen with a purpose.

I. The account of the act of crucifixion is singularly brief, but even in it we find a noteworthy addition, in the statement that Jesus "went out, bearing the cross for Himself." The practice was that the condemned man should carry his cross, and that cruel indignity too was endured by Jesus at the beginning of the short passage to Golgotha, as is shown by John's accurate words, "*went out*, bearing." These perfectly harmonise with, and may almost be said to presuppose, what the other evangelists tell us; that is, that when the sad procession was outside the gate, it was needful to find some one else to carry the burden, which His physical strength sank under. Simon of Cyrene was "coming out of the country," when he was pressed into that service, which suggests that he was met outside the city. The other evangelists give the sequel, which teaches the weakness of Christ's flesh. John gives the first arrangement, which teaches the meek willingness of His spirit.

His bearing His cross, like Isaac's carrying the wood

for his own burning, speaks of patient submission to a Father's will, and gives pathetic meaning to the exhortation to "go forth unto Him without the camp, bearing His reproach." We, too, have sometimes to carry the cross on which we are to be crucified.

John leaves the agents of the crucifixion somewhat indefinite by that vague "they," which, however, is probably to be taken as meaning the persons last named; that is, "the chief priests." Whose hands actually nailed Him to the cross mattered little. Probably the soldiers did it, as executioners, skilled in the art; but the real agents were the priests. The ignorant legionaries were no more guilty than their own hammers. The hands that used them as tools were those really stained with innocent blood. While the plea of Christ's dying prayer for His murderers applied to all concerned, its ample folds covered entirely the ignorant instruments of criminally and partially ignorant rulers.

John touches most slightly on the companions in suffering, omitting their crimes and the taunt implied in the association of such men with Jesus; and omitting, too, the jeers of the one and the penitence of the other, and seeing an unintended but eloquent symbol of Christ's dignity, even in humiliation, in His place in the midst. It had been meant to imply that He was chief in crime; it is a witness to His being the centre of all things, and chief wherever He is—" Him first, Him last, Him midst and without end."

II. The next section tells of the royal proclamation in many tongues, and adds much to the accounts of the other Gospels. John uses the technical Latin word for the inscription, "title"; and he alone tells us that it was fixed on the cross by Pilate's orders, and possibly was written by his own hand. It was the last fling of his malice, directed not against Jesus, but the priests. Like many another scoffer, Pilate did not see that the sharpest edge of his gibe cut himself; for, if he thought the pretensions to royalty of such a poor creature so ludicrous, the more disgrace to the unjust judge who let Him be hung up there to die. Caiaphas, the unworthy high priest, had unconsciously uttered one prophecy. Pilate, the unworthy governor, unconsciously spoke another. "This"—this fainting, bleeding, dying Man—is King, not of Jews only, but of all men, just because He hangs there helpless. The cross is His throne. The crown of thorns will be wreathed round with the many crowns of universal dominion. A rule, compared with which Rome's was limited, vulgar, superficial, and transient, was established then. The Redeemer of men is their King.

The fact of the inscription being in three languages is peculiar to John, for the similar clause in Luke is not genuine. The motive for the triple "title" was, probably, the presence at the passover of foreign-born Jews, to all of whom it was desired to make it legible. But we may permissibly see in this accident another unconscious prophecy. Hebrew was the language of revelation; Latin, the tongue of civil authority and law; Greek, that of philosophy and art. These all find their fulfilment in the Christ, and their highest glory is to proclaim Him. Not only these cultivated languages but the rude speech of tribes who were barbarians then was to be capable of receiving and re-echoing the message of His reign, as has been the case with our own English, the ancestor of which was the speech of unlettered tribes when Pilate wrote, and as has been true in the many tongues which Christ's missionaries have been the first to reduce to writing, for the very purpose of entrusting the name of Christ the King to them.

The vigilance of the priests scented possible danger in the reading of the title by the crowds, and their brusque demand to have it altered shows how they were ready to presume on Pilate's compliance. But, like all who yield what they know they should not give up, he tried to cover his weakness by obstinacy. If he had asserted himself a little sooner, he would have escaped his bad pre-eminence. He did not know what he had written, in imperishable characters, in the record of his deeds; and, while he thought himself announcing with fitting dignity his determination, he was declaring that the black lines he had traced would last for ever. Strange that the awful truth of the ineffaceableness of our deeds should come from his lips! Blessed we if we have learned that He whom Pilate slew will blot out our sins from His book. The characteristic of the whole procedure of Jewish accusers and Roman governor is repeated here. They reject, and he proclaims, the King.

III. The additions in the account of the soldiers dividing His garments are as significant as in the other sections. All tell of parting them and casting lots; but John, who stood there, saw and heard the whole, and fills up the narrative of the Synoptics. There is something very horrible in the matter-of-course way in which the soldiers, as soon as they had finished their grim task, set about securing their booty. They had not nerves easily thrilled by the sight of pain, and could coolly allot a dying man's garments, their perquisites, before his very eyes. The outer garments could be divided among them into four parts, but the inner vestment was all of one piece, and would be ruined if cut. Therefore it was drawn lots for.

The literal correspondence of their proceeding with the words of the twenty-second Psalm, from which Jesus took the bitter cry, "My God, My God, why hast Thou forsaken Me?" seemed to the evangelist a fulfilment of prophecy. No doubt the Psalm came from the heart of a sufferer, whether David or an ideal impersonation of Israel, but equally certainly it contains details which never had been applicable to any sufferer, and in which, if we do not see the foreshadowing of the Prince of sufferers, we can only see tasteless exaggerations. We do not need to construct a theory of prophecy (which only a prophet could do) in order to be sure that unless these and other parts of this Psalm are direct prophecies of the minute details of the sufferings of Jesus, they swing in the air, attached to no one. "These things therefore the soldiers did," says John, as if they were but the blind instruments to fulfil the prophecy. High above all their cruelty and stolid greed we are to see the working out of the purpose of God,—a point of view which does not in the least diminish the freedom or responsibility of the actors.

IV. Another group, as profoundly moved as the soldiers were indifferent, stood by the cross, and the original marks the striking contrast between the weeping friends and the legionaries. Does John mean that there were three women there, or four? There are strong reasons for supposing four; and, if so, the likelihood is that the unnamed sister of Jesus' mother was "the mother of Zebedee's children," which makes the subsequent incident all the more natural and pathetic. Jesus knew that sorrow which accompanies death, the pain of leaving dear ones whom we have sheltered to a rough world; and on His cross His heart not only bore the sins of men, but felt filial care for the mother whom He loved as a son.

His address to Mary as "woman" has no trace of the associations which now cling to the word, while yet it gently warns her that the special relationship is ended, and that henceforth adoring love of her Lord is to take the place of maternal love. Mary's experience of the conflict between earthly and heavenly love was peculiarly sharp, because the same person was the object of both. "Behold thy son!" authoritatively commanded her to think no longer of Him in that relation, and lovingly provided for her another comforter, protector, and object for her affections.

Does He not speak thus to all mourning souls who love Him, bidding them find, and assuring them that they may find, in those who represent Him in the world, solace for their grief and objects for their care? And does not His entrusting of Mary to John illustrate by a tender example how love to Him fits us to carry on His tasks, and makes us, in very blessed and wonderful fashion, His representatives on earth? Happy we if we accept as swiftly and thankfully the offices which He honours us by giving, as did that disciple who left even the cross in order to take Mary to "his own home." So the mother glides out of the Gospels; and the only time we hear of her again is when she is named, after the apostles, as one of the disciples.

V. The last earthly act was to provide for His mother, and, that done, Jesus knew "that all things" were "now finished," and nothing remained but to die. The consciousness of accomplished work calmly fills His mind. That consciousness allows Him to give heed to the physical craving which He had repressed, or, possibly, scarcely felt, while anything remained to be done. Of course, the narrative does not mean that Jesus said "I thirst" in order to carry out the Messianic programme, but that His cry, like all the rest of the passion, was Divinely ordered so as to fulfil the prophecies. It is the last expression of bodily suffering, keenly felt once more, in the cessation of the tension of care for others. His pity and love bore Him above these pangs, but not so completely as to deaden them. He had refused the stupefying draught previously offered, but now He accepted the vinegar, which was meant to refresh, and was given with a touch of human kindness.

The same lips, which were parched with thirst and feebly uttered the complaint, spoke in the next moment, when moistened with the drops from the sponge, the triumphant "It is finished." Mark the absence of specification of what was finished. The indefinite expression is a universal one. All that Jesus had come to do was known by Him to be accomplished. Who of us dare go out of this life of half-done tasks and imperfect service with such a claim on our lips? It far transcends Paul's " I have finished my course." Jesus, and only He, dying, looks back on no defects, departures, or omissions. He has done all that the Father gave Him to do, all that love prompted, all that the world needed. That dying word is like to, but greater than, the voice of the Creator pronouncing that His world was "very good." The Divine ideal of redemption, mightier than that of creation, is accomplished, and that finished work remains for ever, needing no supplement, and tolerating none, but abiding through the ages, the foundation of men's hopes and the assurance of their salvation.

The consciousness of completed work could only be followed by the voluntary death. "He bowed His head," unbent till then, and inclined at last, not by reason of weakness, but by His own will. He "gave up His spirit,"—an expression which is not a mere euphemism for natural death, but distinctly means that the death of Jesus was the act of Jesus. The dark waters were indeed round Him, but could not cover Him till He chose, as some man, standing breast-high in the ocean, might will to bow his head beneath the sullen sea, and so voluntarily let it roll its heavy, sluggish wave above his corpse.

LESSON XXIII

The Dawnings of Faith in the Risen Lord

ST. JOHN xx. 1-18

1. "The first day of the week cometh Mary Magdalene early, when it was yet dark, unto the sepulchre, and seeth the stone taken away from the sepulchre.

2. Then she runneth, and cometh to Simon Peter, and to the other disciple, whom Jesus loved, and saith unto them, They have taken away the Lord out of the sepulchre, and we know not where they have laid Him.

3. Peter therefore went forth, and that other disciple, and came to the sepulchre.

4. So they ran both together: and the other disciple did outrun Peter, and came first to the sepulchre.

5. And he stooping down, and looking in, saw the linen clothes lying; yet went he not in.

6. Then cometh Simon Peter following him, and went into the sepulchre, and seeth the linen clothes lie,

7. And the napkin, that was about His head, not lying with the linen clothes, but wrapped together in a place by itself.

8. Then went in also that other disciple, which came first to the sepulchre, and he saw, and believed.

9. For as yet they knew not the scripture, that He must rise again from the dead.

10. Then the disciples went away again unto their own home.

11. But Mary stood without at the sepulchre weeping: and as she wept, she stooped down, and looked into the sepulchre,

12. And seeth two angels in white sitting, the one at the head, and the other at the feet, where the body of Jesus had lain.

13. And they say unto her, Woman, why weepest thou? She saith unto them, Because they have taken away my Lord, and I know not where they have laid Him.

14. And when she had thus said, she turned herself back, and saw Jesus standing, and knew not that it was Jesus.

15. Jesus saith unto her, Woman, why weepest thou? whom seekest thou? She, supposing Him to be the gardener, saith unto Him, Sir, if thou have borne Him hence, tell me where thou hast laid Him, and I will take Him away.

16. Jesus saith unto her, Mary. She turned herself, and

saith unto Him, Rabboni; which is to say, Master.

17. Jesus saith unto her, Touch Me not; for I am not yet ascended to My Father: but go to My brethren, and say unto them, I ascend unto My Father, and your Father; and to My God, and your God.

18. Mary Magdalene came and told the disciples that she had seen the Lord, and that He had spoken these things unto her."

JOHN'S purpose in his narrative of the resurrection is not only to establish the fact, but also to depict the gradual growth of faith in it, among the disciples. The two main incidents in this lesson, the visit of Peter and John to the tomb and the appearance of our Lord to Mary, give the dawning of faith before sight and the rapturous faith born of sight. In the remainder of the chapter, beyond our lesson, are two more instances of faith following vision, and the teaching of the whole is summed up in Christ's words to the doubter: "Because thou hast seen Me, thou hast believed: blessed are they that have not seen, and yet have believed."

I. The open sepulchre and the bewildered alarm it excited. The act of resurrection took place before sunrise. "At midnight," probably, "the bridegroom came." It was fitting that He who was to scatter the darkness of the grave should rise while darkness covered the earth, and that no eye should behold "how" that dead was "raised up." The earthquake, and the descent of angels, and the rolling away of the stone, were after the tomb was empty.

John's note of time seems somewhat earlier than that of the other Gospels, but is not so much so as to require the supposition that Mary preceded the other women. She appears alone here, because the reason for mention. ing her at all is to explain how Peter and John knew of the empty tomb, and she alone had been the informant.

Dawnings of Faith in the Risen Lord

In these Eastern lands, "as it began to dawn," "very early, at the rising of the sun," and "while it was yet dark," are times very near each other, and Mary may have reached the sepulchre a little before the others. Her own words "we know not" show that she had spoken with others who had seen the empty grave. We must therefore suppose that she had with the others come to it, seen that the sacred corpse was gone and their spices useless, exchanged hurried words of alarm and bewilderment, and then had hastened away, before the appearance of the angels.

The impulse to tell the leaders of the forlorn band the news which she thinks to be so bad was womanly and natural. It was not hope, but wonder and sorrow, that quickened her steps, as she ran through the still morning to find them. Whether they were in one house or not is uncertain; but, at all events, Peter's denial had not cut him off from his brethren, and the two who were so constantly associated before and afterwards were not far apart that morning. The disciple who had stood by the cross to almost the last had an open heart and probably an open house for the denier. "Restore such an one, . . . considering thyself."

Mary had seen the tomb empty, and springs to the conclusion that "they"—some unknown persons—have taken away the dead body, which, with clinging love that tries to ignore death, she still calls "the Lord." Possibly she may have thought that the resting-place in Joseph's new sepulchre was only meant for temporary shelter (ver. 15). At all events, it was gone, and the fact suggested no hope to her. How often do we, in like manner, misinterpret as dark what is really pregnate with light, and blindly attribute to "them" what Jesus does! The tone of mind thus remote from anticipation of the great fact is a precious proof of the historical truth of the resurrection; for here was no soil in which hallucinations would spring, and such people would not have believed Him risen unless they had seen Him living!

II. Peter and John at the tomb, the dawning of faith and the continuance of bewildered wonder. In the account, we may observe, first, the characteristic conduct of each of the two. Peter is first to set out, and John follows, both men doing according to their kind. The younger runs faster than his companion. He looked into the tomb, and saw the wrappings lying; but the reverent awe which holds back finer natures kept him from venturing in. Peter is not said to have looked before entering. He loved with all his heart, but his love was impetuous and practical, and he went straight in, and felt no reason why he should pause. His boldness encouraged his friend, as the example of strong natures does. Most of my readers will recall Bushnell's noble sermon on "Unconscious Influence," from this incident, and need no more about it.

Observe, too, the further witness of the folded graveclothes. John from outside had not seen the napkin, lying carefully rolled up apart from the other cloths. It was probably laid in a part of the tomb invisible from without. But the order of these came to him, when he saw them, with a great flash of illumination. There had been no hurried removal.

Here had been no hostile hands, or there would not have been this deliberation; nor friendly hands, or there would not have been such dishonour to the sacred dead as to carry away the body nude. What did it mean? Could He Himself have done for Himself what He had bade them do for Lazarus? Could He have laid aside the garments of the grave as needing them no more? "They have taken away,"—what if it were not "they," but He? No trace of hurry or struggle was there. He did "not go out with haste, nor go by flight," but calmly, deliberately, in the majesty of His lordship over death, He rose from His slumber and left order in the land of confusion.

Observe, too, the birth of the apostle's faith. John connects it with the sight of the folded garments. "Believed" here must mean more than recognition of the fact that the grave was empty. The next clause seems to imply that it means belief in the resurrection. The scripture, which they "knew" as scripture, was for John suddenly interpreted, and he was lifted out of the ignorance of its meaning, which till that moment he had shared with his fellow-disciples. Their failure to understand Christ's frequent distinct prophecies that He would rise again the third day has been thought incredible, but is surely intelligible enough if we remember how unexampled such a thing was, and how marvellous is our power of hearing, and yet not hearing, the plainest truth. We all in the course of our lives are lost in astonishment, when things befall us which we have been plainly told will befall. The fulfilment of all Divine promises (and threatenings) is a surprise, and no warnings beforehand teach one tithe so clearly as experience.

John believed, but Peter still was in the dark. Again the former had outrun his friend. His more sensitive nature, not to say his deeper love,—for that would be unjust, since their love differed in quality more than in degree,—had gifted him with a more subtle and swifter-working perception. Perhaps if Peter's heart had not been oppressed by his sin, he would have been readier to feel the sunshine of the wonderful hope. We condemn ourselves to the shade when we deny our Lord by deed or word.

III. The first appearance of the Lord, and revelation of the new form of intercourse. Nothing had been said of Mary's return to the tomb; but how could she stay away? The disciples might go, but she lingered, woman-like, to indulge in the bitter-sweet of tears. Eyes so filled are more apt to see angels. No wonder that these calm watchers, in their garb of purity and joy, had not been seen by the two men. The laws of such appearance are not those of ordinary optics. Spiritual susceptibility and need determine who shall see angels, and who shall see but the empty place. Wonder and adoration held these bright forms there. They had hovered over the cradle and stood by the shepherds at Bethlehem, but they bowed in yet more awestruck reverence at the grave, and death revealed to them a deeper depth of Divine love.

The presence of angels was a trifle to Mary, who had only one thought,—the absence of her Lord. Surely that touch of her unmoved answer, as if speaking to men, is beyond the reach of art. She says "*My* Lord" now, and "*I* know not," but otherwise repeats her former words, untouched by any hope caught from John. Her clinging love needed more than an empty grave and folded clothes and waiting angels to stay its tears, and

Dawnings of Faith in the Risen Lord

she turned indifferently and wearily away from the interruption of the question to plunge again into her sorrow. Chrysostom suggests that she "turned herself," because she saw in the angels' looks that they saw Christ suddenly appearing behind her; but the preceding explanation seems better. Her not knowing Jesus might be accounted for by her absorbing grief. One who looked at white-robed angels, and saw nothing extraordinary, would give but a careless glance at the approaching figure, and might well fail to recognise Him. But probably, as in the case of the two travellers to Emmaus, her "eyes were holden," and the cause of non-recognition was not so much a change in Jesus as an operation on her.

Be that as it may, it is noteworthy that His voice, which was immediately to reveal Him, at first suggested nothing to her; and even His gentle question, with the significant addition to the angels' words, in "Whom seekest thou?" which indicated His knowledge that her tears fell for some person dear and lost, only made her think of Him as being the gardener, and therefore probably concerned in the removal of the body. If He were so, He would be friendly; and so she ventured her pathetic petition, which does not name Jesus (so full is her mind of the one, that she thinks everybody must know whom she means), and which so overrated her own strength in saying "I will take Him away." The first words of the risen Christ are on His lips yet to all sad hearts. He seeks our confidences, and would have us tell Him the occasions of our tears. He would have us recognise that all our griefs and all our desires point to one person,—Himself,—as the one real object of our "seeking," whom finding, we need weep no more.

Verse sixteen tells us that Mary turned herself to see Him when He next spoke, so that, at the close of her first answer to Him, she must have once more resumed her gaze into the tomb, as if she despaired of the new-comer giving the help she had asked.

Who can say anything about that transcendent recognition, in which all the stooping love of the risen Lord is smelted into one word, and the burst of rapture, awe, astonishment, and devotion pours itself through the narrow channel of one other? If this narrative is the work of some anonymous author late in the second century, he is indeed a "great unknown," and has managed to imagine one of the two or three most pathetic "situations" in literature. Surely it is more reasonable to suppose him no obscure genius, but a well-known recorder of what he had seen, and knew for fact. Christ's calling by name ever reveals His loving presence. We may be sure that He knows us by name, and we should reply with the same swift cry of absolute submission as sprang to Mary's lips. "Rabboni! Master!" is the fit answer to His call.

But Mary's exclamation was imperfect in that it expressed the resumption of no more than the old bond, and her gladness needed enlightenment. Things were not to be as they had been. Christ's "Mary" had indeed assured her of His faithful remembrance and of her present place in His love; but when she clung to His feet she was seeking to keep what she had to learn to give up. Therefore Jesus, who invited the touch which was to establish faith and banish doubt (Luke xxiv.

39; John xx. 27), bids her unclasp her hands, and gently instils the ending of the blessed past by opening to her the superior joys of the begun future. His words contain for us all the very heart of our possible relation to Him, and teach us that we need envy none who companied with Him here. His ascension to the Father is the condition of our truest approach to Him. His prohibition encloses a permission. "Touch Me not; for I am not yet ascended," implies "When I am, you may."

Further, the ascended Christ is still our Brother. Neither the mystery of death nor the impending mystery of dominion broke the tie. Again, the resurrection is the beginning of ascension, and is only then rightly understood when it is considered as the first upward step to the throne. "I ascend," not "I have risen, and will soon leave you," as if the ascension only began forty days after on Olivet. It is already in process. Once more the ascended Christ, our Brother still, and capable of the touch of reverent love, yet is separated from us by the character, even while united to us by the fact, of His filial and dependent relation to God. He cannot say "Our Father" as if standing on the common human ground. He is Son, as we are not, and we are sons through Him, and can only call God our Father because He is Christ's.

Such were the immortal hopes and new thoughts which Mary hastened from the presence of her recovered Lord to bring to the disciples. Fragrant though but partially understood, they were like half-opened blossoms from the tree of life planted in the midst of that garden, to bloom unfading, and ever disclosing new beauty in believing hearts till the end of time.

LESSON XXIV

The Sea and the Shore

ST. JOHN xxi. 1-14

1. "After these things Jesus showed Himself again to the disciples at the sea of Tiberias; and on this wise showed He Himself.

2. There were together Simon Peter, and Thomas called Didymus, and Nathanael of Cana in Galilee, and the sons of Zebedee, and two other of His disciples.

3. Simon Peter saith unto them, I go a fishing. They say unto him, We also go with thee. They went forth, and entered into a ship immediately; and that night they caught nothing.

4. But when the morning was now come, Jesus stood on the shore: but the disciples knew not that it was Jesus.

5. Then Jesus saith unto them, Children, have ye any meat? They answered Him, No.

6. And He said unto them, Cast the net on the right side of the ship, and ye shall find. They cast therefore, and now they were not able to draw it for the multitude of fishes.

7. Therefore that disciple whom Jesus loved saith unto Peter, It is the Lord. Now when Simon Peter heard that it was the Lord, he girt his fisher's coat unto him, (for he was naked,) and did cast himself into the sea.

8. And the other disciples came in a little ship; (for they were not far from land, but as it were two hundred cubits,) dragging the net with fishes.

9. As soon then as they were come to land, they saw a fire of coals there, and fish laid thereon, and bread.

10. Jesus saith unto them, Bring of the fish which ye have now caught.

11. Simon Peter went up, and drew the net to land full of great fishes, an hundred and fifty and three: and for all there were so many, yet was not the net broken.

12. Jesus saith unto them, Come and dine. And none of the disciples durst ask Him, Who art Thou? knowing that it was the Lord.

13. Jesus then cometh, and taketh bread, and giveth them, and fish likewise.

14. This is now the third time that Jesus showed Himself to His disciples, after that He was risen from the dead."

The Sea and the Shore

THE last chapter of this Gospel is obviously an appendix by the author. The last verses of chapter xx. are clearly intended as the conclusion of the whole, and, as clearly, chapter xxi. is by the same hand as the former. It falls into two parts,—the former setting forth the work of the Church as a whole, and the latter the varying tasks of individuals. The former is our lesson, which is parted off from the second half by the notice in verse fourteen.

I. We note the little group and their night of toil. The catalogue is significant. There are seven of the disciples together, and the fact that they were together implies the resurrection. What stopped the disintegrating process which began at Calvary? Why had not the sheep scattered when the Shepherd was smitten? They would certainly have sought safety in flight, and buried their shattered illusions and hopes in isolation, unless some powerful magnet had drawn them together. It is no exaggeration to say that the holding together of the apostles after the crucifixion is not the least cogent proof of the resurrection.

The fact that they were in Galilee is significant. Jesus had bid them go; and by the narration of this incident John unites the cycle of appearances of the risen Lord in Jerusalem and in Galilee, which are recorded separately in the Synoptics. Nor is the composition of the company unimportant. As a whole, it is the reproduction of the original nucleus mentioned in chapter i. Peter, John, and Nathanael are named here; and the conjecture that the remaining two of the first five disciples—namely, Andrew and Philip—are the anonymous two of this narrative seems reasonable. If so, all who had been at the beginning were recipients of this "manifestation," with the addition of Thomas and James, who make up the number of completeness, the symbolic seven, which indicates the representative character of the group.

The individuals are significant, as is the order of mention. First comes Peter, not merely because he was usually foremost; for he is associated with Thomas, the denier with the doubter, as if the two greatest sinners were put first, the more to enhance the love which drew near to them. Then comes Nathanael, the guileless, who had been seeing ever greater things during all the Lord's ministry, and had never been heard of again since that first day. He is the type of quiet growth, silent advance in vision, and Christ-like guilelessness. Then come the sons of Zebedee, John hiding himself as much as possible, according to his wont. Who but himself would have put him in that place? It is an unmistakable sign of his authorship. Then come the two anonymous disciples, who had nothing to make their names worth handing down, but yet were worthy to see the Lord on the shore. Commonplace people, with no special brilliancy of gifts or distinguished capacity of service, are none the worse for obscurity, and see the Master just as well.

Peter is leader as usual. His purpose to "go a-fishing" was welcomed by the others. It was no despairing return to their old trade, as if the high hopes with which they had left it were all gone to water, but the calm occupation of themselves with wholesome toil, while with patience waiting for the promised presence of Jesus. The best way of spending times of expectation of great events is in the discharge of small ordinary duties. To fishers at their work Jesus manifests Himself.

II. What befell them at sea. The long night of fruitless toil perhaps may have reminded some of them of the other similar experience; but, more probably, they were too busy and weary to think of anything but their empty nets. Whether they remembered that first miraculous draught of fishes or no, we must keep it constantly in view, if we would understand this incident, and must remember that our Lord Himself gave it a symbolical meaning. The whole of the events in this lesson point to that symbolism as a chief part of the intention; and, while it is easy to be over-ingenious in translating the facts into parables, it is unwise to shut our eyes to the broad features which receive their full meaning only when so translated.

As the day was breaking over the Eastern girdling hills, and the cold air at sunrise telling of a change in the dark world, Jesus stood on the shore. The place is significant,—the disciples tossing on the water, the Lord standing on the firm beach, with the light playing round Him. Can we fail to see in that the picture of the condition of His servants in contrast with the rest and stable glory where He dwells? And may we not see in His attitude the same inspiring truth which upheld Stephen dying, when he saw the Son of Man in the opened heaven, standing as ready to help? The disciples did not recognise Him. Throughout the forty days His will determined when He should be known.

The Unknown speaks as a superior, using the address "Children," and His question in the original implies the expectation of a "No." "Then you have not anything to eat?" He knew the state of things before asking, but He wished the acknowledgment. Is not that ever His procedure with His servants, drawing them to confess their failure, and so preparing them for the blessing, which He cannot send except to the consciously weak and powerless? An honest and humble "No" is generally followed by correction of methods or fields, and that by full nets. If we said it more readily to Him who is ever interested in our work, we should not have to say it so often to ourselves.

The prompt obedience to the Stranger's directions was probably due to the disciples' belief that He had seen from the shore some sign of a shoal which they in the twilight had not noticed. None of them had any thought of His being anything more than a passing traveller, stopping to look on. The swift result is, alas! not always the experience of even the humblest and most docile of Christ's servants; but we may be sure that, though in regard to immediate issues the parable of this incident may fail, it does not fail in regard to their certainty. Jesus did not promise them that they should find at once, nor does He promise us; but He does promise that, sooner or later, our labour will not be "in vain," if it be "in the Lord." And that may content us.

The beautiful episode of Peter and John is full of meaning. Love has quick eyes, and is first to discern the Christ. Its prerogative is to trace His working where others do not see Him; and for love it is enough to know that "it is the Lord," and to sit quietly blessed in contemplation. But there is another kind of faithful devotion, not so quick to discern, but eager to act. John could sit still, satisfied to gaze, but Peter flung his upper garment about him, and was over the side and splashing in the water before he knew what he was doing. He was only a hundred yards off, and would have been by Jesus almost as soon if he had sat still; but that was not his way, and "there are diversities of operations." Besides, penitence and the blended shame and joy of restoration made him flounder thus quickly to his Lord. He had said, "Depart from me; for I am a sinful man, O Lord," on that first similar occasion; but the sense of sin which drives to Jesus is deeper and wholesomer than that which drives from Him. The safest place for the forgiven penitent is close to the Lord.

III. What befell on the shore. If the sea is the symbol of this unquiet world, and the night of toil ended by the securing the fish, that of the Church's work as fishers of men, the stable shore and what happened there must be the symbol of the rest that remaineth for the people of God. Who kindled that mysterious fire, or whence came the fish and bread, we cannot tell. But its meaning is clear enough. Not only may it teach us how even here Jesus provides seasons of refreshing repose for wearied servants, and cares for their need, but it prophesies of the repast which He prepares hereafter for them; and that aspect of the meal gives significance to the command to bring of the fish now caught. For in that world of rest we shall eat the fruit of our doings, and the results of Christian service are parts of the provision of His table in His kingdom.

Peter is again first to haul in the net. An eye-witness speaks in the precise enumeration of number and specification that they were "great fishes." Fantastic explanations of these points have been given, which need not be repeated, but the unbroken net may be meant to teach that all Christ's true servants will be landed on that peaceful shore.

Jesus invites His disciples to the meal, but they hold back in awe. There the parallel fails; for then the profounder the reverence, the closer the approach, and in the sunlit certainties of the land where we shall see Him as He is, none of the disciples will need to ask, Who art Thou? knowing that it is the Lord. Then He Himself will come forth and serve His feasting servants, according to His own promise, and as He did on that morning by the lake. For us, too, the scene of our labours, failures, and darkened nights of toil and weeping will lie sleeping in the morning sunlight, and from the Lord's own hands we shall receive the blessed results which His grace has given to issue from our poor service, mingled with the yet more blessed and glorious issues, with which we have nothing to do but to receive them at His hands.

LESSON XXV

Review Lesson Thoughts

THE passion week occupies nearly half of this Gospel. Why should it? The answer will carry us far into the mystery of the Cross, which thus throws its shadow, or rather its light, over so wide a field.

Lessons XIII. and XIV. are preliminary to the main theme. The raising of Lazarus was closely connected with the crucifixion, as the excitement it produced steeled and precipitated the rulers' resolution. It casts light on the Cross, by the strange contrast between Jesus as giving life to the dead and Himself dying.

The narrative brings out three phases in the self-revelation of Jesus,—His dignity, as expressed in His majestic promise to the sisters; His declaration, impossible to sane human lips, that He is resurrection and life, in whom, believing, dead men live, and, living, never die; His authoritative questioning as to faith in Him, and His acceptance of the twofold title of the Christ and Son of God. The second phase is that of His sharing in the true human emotions of sorrow and indignation at the ravages of sin, His troubles and tears. The third is His Divine, life-giving power, breaking the fetters with a word. He weeps, and He says, " Lazarus, come forth." To know Him aright, we must take both into account. To understand the Cross, we must remember the grave of Lazarus.

Lesson XIV. gives a further preparation for that central mystery of love, by teaching us to look at Christ's death with His eyes. So beheld it is wondrously transfigured, and becomes radiant with glory,—the condition of His bringing forth much fruit, the pattern to which the lives of all true servants must conform, since only followers are reckoned servants. But amid all the glorious anticipations there blends the minor key of human shrinking, and the calm spirit is troubled, and flesh prompts the cry for escape; but the unfaltering will and unwavering love to us keep Him from yielding to the innocent recoil from death. The heavenly Voice answered the filial prayer, and once more the visions of what His death would do filled His thoughts. It was to be the judgment of the world, the casting out of the world's Prince,—the all-attractive magnet to bring hearts to Him, drawn by the all-subduing forces of His sacrifice. There is but one conception of Christ's death, which saves these visions from the name of fond delusions, and delivers Him from the charge of going to His death with a false idea of His own importance; and that is the belief that He died the sacrifice for the sins of the world.

Lessons XV. to XIX. carry us to the upper room, that simple chamber on the roof, which by these few hours has become for all time "the holy place of the tabernacles of the Most High." First came a deed of transcendent love, fitly followed by the inexhaustible words of comfort and teaching; and these, again, lead up to the great prayer, than which the speech of earth can utter, and the ears of mortals hear, nothing more sacred. Silent adoration is more to the purpose than many words.

In Lesson XV. the central truth is that of Jesus as servant, and of cleansing as His lowliest, loftiest service. The sweet and wondrous story is preceded by a profound exposition of its motives, from which we learn that even Christ's love was capable of increasing tenderness, and that He too felt the truly human impulse to make last moments specially full of tokens of love. The consciousness of His Divine origin, authority, and destination moved Him to the lowly garb and act of the attendant slave. So His humiliation became a revelation of His exaltation, and in it He taught us the right use of felt power and superiority. How different the world and we should be if we laid that lesson to heart! The act of service reminds us, as in a sensible symbol, of the emptying Himself of His garments of glory, but is yet more impressive and touching in its literality than as a symbol. This unclothed, stooping Man, washing the dusty feet, and taking their foulness on to the cloth that wrapped Himself, is the incarnate God. Who can say anything worthy? The lesson of cleansing, as essential to participation in Him, needs no enforcement, nor the teaching that this lowly act of His is the law for us. What they need is that we should live as if we believed them, and should not be content with admiring the story, but should follow it.

The sweet and deep consolations of the three succeeding lessons scarcely admit of summarising; but we should try to grasp firmly the main thought of each.

That of Lesson XVI. seems to be the great truth that the absent Christ is present with all who love Him, and that through the Divine Spirit. "Let not your heart be troubled" gives the purpose of the whole. "Believe also in Me" shows how troubled hearts may be calmed and solitary ones companioned. His absence is but in continuation of the design of His presence. He has gone before us to prepare the many mansions of the Father's house, just as, if we may say so, the two disciples had gone before the rest to prepare the chamber where they were. Separation for such a purpose means reunion. The permanent presence of the Advocate, the Spirit of strength, is assured to all Christians, and in that presence Jesus Himself comes to us. "Presence" and "absence" are delusive words when applied to the relations between us and our Lord. No Christian has any right to think of Jesus as away from him. He comes by His Spirit, and we can bring and keep Him by keeping His word. Then He will make His abode with us.

Lesson XVII. sets forth the indissoluble union, independent of "place," between Christ and us, by the parable of the vine. The main idea in it is the unity of life between Christ and us. That unity is not to be weakened and watered down into metaphor. The life of Jesus Christ does move in every Christian spirit, as truly as the vine's sap permeates every blushing cluster and tiny twig. We are fruitful only in the measure in which it permeates us. But that unity is of a higher kind than vegetative oneness, which does not mean that it is less real. A branch can depart from this Vine, and there must be the conscious effort to abide. How do we resist the tendency to separation? By letting His words abide in us (John xv. 7), and keeping His commandments (John xv. 10). And what are His commandments? They are all one,—love (John xv. 12). And what are the results of abiding? Fruit, true discipleship, the abiding in us of His perfect joy, filling our hearts, the possession of His confidence, insight into His doings, His friendship, and the power of reception of all that we desire when our desires are abiding in Him.

Lesson XVIII. expands the promise of the Spirit as the continual possession of believers, and that especially in two ways, as convicting the world by the ministry of Christians, and as teaching the Church. In regard to their defenceless position in a hostile world, Christians are to fall back trustfully on the assurance that they have an unfailing Helper, who, through them, will carry on the great plea against the world. The world's sin is mainly manifest in its unbelief in Him. What must He have been who could set that at the head of the catalogue of sins? A righteousness which may be the world's is revealed by the ascension and glory of the Crucified, and a judgment which will crush sin, if it have not been cleansed by accepting Christ's righteousness, is established by the fact that already in the Cross the Prince of the world has been cast out. These three truths are the staple of the Church's message, and will be victorious in proportion as we hold to them, and proclaim them in dependence on the convincing Spirit. His work lies within the Church as well as on the world by the Church; and step by step He guides docile souls into all truth concerning Jesus, glorifying Him as

Jesus has glorified the Father. This teaching Spirit is with us if we are abiding in Christ.

The unapproachable sanctity of the intercessory prayer bids us listen in silence. Jesus prays for Himself. Note His petition, that He may be glorified; its purpose not His own advantage, but ours, attained by His glorifying of the Father; its grounds, namely, that His return to His eternal glory is the completion of the gifts and mission already His (vers. 2, 3), and the fit reward of His work (ver. 4). Then comes the prayer for the disciples, which is summed in that one petition, "keep." That prayer, like the former, is grounded on two thoughts,—the genuine though imperfect discipleship of His disciples (vers. 6-10), and their desolation when left by Him (ver. 11). To be kept "in the Name" is the true security and blessedness. It is Christ's desire for us, if we are His. This prayer was the beginning of His continual intercession. Like the mighty angel of the Apocalypse, He stands here, as with one foot on the sea of time and the other on the eternal shore, and lifts up the voice which God heareth always, for us tossing on the billows. The glorified Christ is the interceding Christ.

Lessons XX. and XXI. go together, as the arrest and trial. The chief point in the former is the revelation of Christ's voluntary surrender to force which by one flash of His will He could paralyse. The contrast between such power kept by Him sheathed and idle, and Peter's foolish brandishing of his useless weapon, heightens the impression of the Lord's meek submission, while His words to the soldiers express the motive for His submission to suffering and death so distinctly that they need no change in order to set forth the very heart of His redeeming work: "If ye seek Me, let these go their way."

The next lesson is more occupied with Pilate and rulers than with Jesus, and that very fact is eloquent of His meek patience, as a lamb silent before its shearers. Three types of character appear united against Jesus. The rude soldiers mock, and their mockery turns to honour and prophecies. Pilate is self-interested, irresolute, troubled by suspicions that this is no common man, and certainly no malefactor. But he gets no answer to his question, because he had not heeded former answers to former ones, was stifling convictions, and doing violence to conscience for personal advantage. His taunts at the Jews and their helpless King told how ill at ease he was, and how degraded in his own eyes by cowardly compliance with a howling mob. The bitter enmity of the rulers drove them on to deny their King, and to be false to their national hopes. They hated Jesus so much that they swore loyalty to Tiberius. Christ, or tyrants, is the alternative for us too.

John's account of the crucifixion is intended to emphasise the calm majesty of the dying Christ, and to point to His cross as His regal throne. Hence he tells of the central place between the malefactors, and not of the scoffs of one of them, and dwells on the fact that the inscription was set by Pilate's order, and that it proclaimed Christ's royalty in the three languages which divided the civilised world; and that it not only proclaimed His royalty as His claim, but as a fact, and that it was a permanent record. Hence, too, he tells of the rent garments and unrent robe, and points to the minute correspondence of the details with the Psalm in which a royal sufferer of old had spoken. Hence he tells, hiding himself, of the calmness of loving care which had entrusted him with the precious bequest of the mother of the Lord; and hence he tells how, with that last act of thoughtful filial love, Jesus felt His mission done, and, in triumphant consciousness of a finished work, willed to die, and bowing His head, which drooped because He bowed it, died, and therein proved Himself the Lord of death and life.

The two scenes from the resurrection morning illustrate the growth of the disciples' faith in the risen Lord. The evangelist hides his own personality, but he tells that he was the first to believe in the resurrection; and his narrative, so vivid and minute, shows how that morning lived in his memory. The first faith in Christ's resurrection came not from sight, but from the evidence of the empty tomb, the folded grave-clothes, and the flash of light upon "the Scripture," which these brought to John. He outran Peter and them all in faith; and though Peter was first in the tomb, his companion was first to understand the meaning of what met them there. The second believer in the resurrection was the first beholder of the risen Lord. But it was not sight, but hearing, that revealed Him; and we may be sure that hearing would have been as ineffectual as sight, unless He had willed to be known. We cannot tell why Jesus chose to be seen first by Mary, unless we take the other evangelist's hint, "out of whom He had cast seven devils," as supplying the reason, in that she owed so much and loved so much; but we can lay to heart the teaching as to the possibility of more blessed intercourse with the ascended Lord than any clasping of His feet here could ever bring, and may thankfully and humbly claim the brotherhood with Him on His throne, and the participation with Him in the Fatherhood of His Father and ours, which He has given to us all, when He gave them to the kneeling woman.

The last scene by the lake in the morning light is clearly best understood as being a prophetical repetition, with significant differences, of the first miraculous draught of fishes, directed not only, as that was, to impressing by symbol the conditions of service on the future fishers of men, but also, while confirming the lessons of that earlier scene, going beyond it, in its blessed symbols of the reward. The fire on the shore, the presence of the recognised Lord in the breaking morning, the various ways by which the disciples reach the beach, the firm shore itself, the refreshment prepared, the command to bring the fish they had caught, the meal at which Jesus is the servant, all point on to the result and reward of His servants' toil, when they "rest from their labours," by the fire which His own hands have kindled on the eternal shore, and "their works do follow them," inasmuch as they are bidden "to bring of the fish which they had caught."

THE EXPOSITOR'S BIBLE.

EDITED BY REV.

W. ROBERTSON NICOLL, M.A., LL.D.

FIRST SERIES.

Price 7s. 6d. each Volume.

THE BOOK OF GENESIS.

By the Rev. Professor *MARCUS DODS, D.D.*

SIXTH EDITION.

THE FIRST BOOK OF SAMUEL.
THE SECOND BOOK OF SAMUEL.

By the Rev. Professor *W. G. BLAIKIE, D.D., LL.D.*

FOURTH EDITION, TWO VOLS.

"Very full of suggestive thought."—*English Churchman.*
"A solid and able piece of work."—*Academy.*

THE GOSPEL OF ST. MARK.

By the Very Rev. *G. A. CHADWICK, D.D.*, Dean of Armagh.

FOURTH EDITION.

"This exposition is original, full of life, striking, and relevant. He has given us the fruit of much careful thought."—*British Weekly.*

THE EPISTLES TO THE COLOSSIANS AND PHILEMON.

By the Rev. *ALEXANDER MACLAREN, D.D.*

FIFTH EDITION.

"In nothing Dr. Maclaren has written is there more of beauty, of spiritual insight, or of brilliant elucidation of Scripture. Indeed, Dr. Maclaren is here at his best."—*Expositor.*

THE EPISTLE TO THE HEBREWS.

By the Rev. Principal *T. C. EDWARDS, D.D.*

FOURTH EDITION.

"There is abundant evidence of accurate scholarship, acute criticism, patient thought, and faculty of lucid exposition. However thoroughly any one has studied the Epistle here explained, he will certainly find in Dr. Edwards' volume fresh suggestions."—*Dr. Marcus Dods.*

THE EXPOSITOR'S BIBLE.

SECOND SERIES.

Price 7s. 6d. each Volume.

THE BOOK OF ISAIAH.
Vol. I. Chapters I.-XXXIX.
By the Rev. GEORGE ADAM SMITH, M.A.

SIXTH EDITION.

"This is a very attractive book. Mr. George Adam Smith had evidently such a mastery of the scholarship of his subject that it would be a sheer impertinence for most scholars, even though tolerable Hebraists, to criticise his translations. . . . A lucid, impressive, and vivid study of Isaiah."—*Spectator.*

THE EPISTLE TO THE GALATIANS.
By the Rev. Professor G. G. FINDLAY, B.A.

THIRD EDITION.

"In this volume we have the mature results of broad and accurate scholarship, exegetical tact, and a firm grasp of the great principles underlying the Gospel of Paul presented in a form so lucid and attractive that every thoughtful reader can enjoy it."—*Dr. Beet.*

THE EPISTLES OF ST. JOHN.
By the Right Rev. W. ALEXANDER, D.D., D.C.L., Lord Bishop of Derry and Raphoe.

SECOND EDITION.

"Full of felicities of exegesis. . . . Brilliant and valuable."—*Literary Churchman.*

FIRST EPISTLE TO CORINTHIANS.
By the Rev. Professor MARCUS DODS, D.D.

THIRD EDITION.

"Dr. Dods' writings are always excellent, and the one before us is no exception to the rule."—*Record.*

THE BOOK OF REVELATION.
By the Rev. Professor W. MILLIGAN, D.D.

SECOND EDITION.

"Dr. Milligan's scholarly and attractive exposition."—*Aberdeen Free Press.*

THE PASTORAL EPISTLES.
By the Rev. ALFRED PLUMMER, D.D., Durham.

THIRD EDITION.

"The treatment is throughout scholarlike, lucid, thoughtful."—*Guardian.*

THE EXPOSITOR'S BIBLE.
THIRD SERIES.
Price 7s. 6d. each Volume.

THE GOSPEL OF ST. MATTHEW.
By the Rev. *J. MONRO GIBSON, D.D.*

SECOND EDITION.

"This running commentary upon St. Matthew's Gospel sets before the reader our Lord's words, deeds, and sufferings as recorded by that Evangelist in a vivid light."—*Guardian.*

THE BOOK OF EXODUS.
By the Very Rev. *G. A. CHADWICK, D.D.*

SECOND EDITION.

"This is, to a great extent, a model of what an expository commentary should be. To exhibit the Old Testament in the light of the New, and to point out the spiritual and permanent truth under the type by which it was in that early age expressed, and through which it still shines, cannot fail to render a commentary extremely valuable."—*Literary Churchman.*

JUDGES AND RUTH.
By the Rev. *R. A. WATSON, M.A.*, Author of "Gospels of Yesterday."

"This is an unusually attractive volume. His pages will give many a valuable hint to the preacher."—*Literary Churchman.*

THE GOSPEL OF ST. LUKE.
By the Rev. *HENRY BURTON, M.A.*

"His chapters are full of vivid illustration, and fresh, bright exposition."
—*Record.*

THE PROPHECIES OF JEREMIAH.
With a Sketch of His Life and Times.

By the Rev. *C. J. BALL, M.A.*, Chaplain of Lincoln's Inn.

"The critical portion will be prized most as it exhibits deep learning, breadth of view, and clear insight into the prophet's meaning."—*Manchester Examiner.*

THE BOOK OF ISAIAH.
Vol. II. By the Rev. *GEORGE ADAM SMITH, M.A.*

SECOND EDITION.

"The results of thorough scientific study are here presented, not as the bare and wintry stem which too often repels, but rich and attractive, with the foliage and fruit which sound criticism yields."—*Dr. Marcus Dods.*

THE EXPOSITOR'S BIBLE.

FOURTH SERIES.

Price 7s. 6d. each Volume.

THE GOSPEL OF ST. JOHN. VOL. I.

By the Rev. *MARCUS DODS, D.D.*, Professor of Exegetical Theology, New College, Edinburgh.

"An excellent contribution to the series. Dr. Dods has the gift of lucidity of expression."—*Guardian.*

THE EPISTLES OF ST. JAMES AND ST. JUDE.

By the Rev. *A. PLUMMER, D.D.*, Master of University College, Durham.

"It is even a better piece of work than his former volume on the Pastoral Epistles. It contains everything that the student can desire by way of introduction to the two Epistles, while for those who read with an eye to the manufacture of sermons, or for their own edification, the doctrinal and moral lessons are developed in a style redolent of books, yet singularly easy and unaffected. Points of interest abound."—*Saturday Review.*

THE BOOK OF ECCLESIASTES.

With a New Translation.

By the Rev. *SAMUEL COX, D.D.*

"The most luminous, original, and practical exposition of Ecclesiastes which is within the reach of ordinary English readers."—*Speaker.*

THE BOOK OF PROVERBS.

By the Rev. *R. F. HORTON, M.A.*, Hampstead.

"In each of these lectures will be found much strong and vigorous thought, firm and logical reasoning, and the results of high culture and ability."—*Literary Churchman.*

THE BOOK OF LEVITICUS.

By the Rev. *S. H. KELLOGG, D.D.*, Author of "The Light of Asia and the Light of the World."

"He has certainly succeeded in investing with fresh interest this old book of laws, with whose spirit he seems so heartily in sympathy.'—*Scotsman.*

THE ACTS OF THE APOSTLES. VOL. I.

By the Rev. Professor *G. T. STOKES, D.D.*

"A very valuable addition to Biblical literature."—*British Weekly.*

THE EXPOSITOR'S BIBLE.

FIFTH SERIES, 1891—92.

Price 7s. 6d. each Volume.

THE BOOK OF JOB.
By the Rev. *R. A. WATSON, D.D.*, Author of "Gospels of Yesterday," etc.

THE EPISTLES TO THE THESSA-LONIANS.
By the Rev. *JAMES DENNEY, B.D.*

THE PSALMS. VOL. I.
By the Rev. *ALEXANDER MACLAREN, D.D.*

THE ACTS OF THE APOSTLES. VOL. II.
By the Rev. Professor *G. T. STOKES, D.D.*

THE EPISTLE TO THE EPHESIANS.
By the Rev. Professor *G. G. FINDLAY, B.A.*

THE GOSPEL OF ST. JOHN. VOL. II.
By the Rev. Professor *MARCUS DODS, D.D*

THE EXPOSITOR'S BIBLE.

SIXTH SERIES.

Price 7s. 6d. each volume.

THE EPISTLE TO THE PHILIPPIANS.
By the Rev. Principal *RAINY, D.D.*

THE FIRST BOOK OF KINGS.
By the Ven. Archdeacon *FARRAR, D.D., F.R.S.*

EZRA, NEHEMIAH, AND ESTHER.
By the Rev. Professor *W. F. ADENEY, M.A.*

THE BOOK OF JOSHUA.
By the Rev. Professor *W. G. BLAIKIE, D.D., LL.D.*

THE BOOK OF DANIEL.
By the Rev. Professor *J. M. FULLER, M.A.*

THE BOOK OF PSALMS. VOL. II.
By the Rev. *ALEXANDER MACLAREN, D.D.*

WORKS BY THE REV. DR. FAIRBAIRN.

I.

THE CITY OF GOD.

A Series of Discussions in Religion.

By the Rev. *A. M. FAIRBAIRN*, D.D., Principal of Mansfield College, Oxford.

THIRD EDITION.

Price 7s. 6d.

CONTENTS:—Faith and Modern Thought—Theism and Science—Man and Religion—God and Israel—The Problem of Job—Man and God—The Jesus of History and the Christ of Faith—Christ in History—The Riches of Christ's Poverty—The Quest of the Chief Good—Love of Christ—The City of God.

"We find in the discourses which form this volume much able statement and much vigorous thought, and an admirable comprehension of the great questions which are being discussed in our day with eagerness and bated breath."—*Scotsman.*

II.

STUDIES IN THE LIFE OF CHRIST.

FIFTH EDITION.

Demy 8vo, price 9s.

CONTENTS:—The Historical Conditions—The Narratives of the Birth and Infancy—The Growth and Education of Jesus—His Personality—The Baptist and the Christ—The Temptation of Christ—The New Teacher—The Kingdom of Heaven—Galilee, Judea, Samaria—The Master and the Disciples—The Earlier Miracles—Jesus and the Jews—The Later Teaching—The Later Miracles—Jericho and Jerusalem—Gethsemane—The Betrayer—The Chief Priests—The Trial—The Crucifixion—The Resurrection.

"There is ample room for Professor Fairbairn's thoughtful and brilliant sketches. Dr. Fairbairn's is not the base rhetoric often employed to hide want of thought or poverty of thought, but the noble rhetoric which is alive with thought and imagination to its utmost and finest extremities."
—*Expositor.*

THE CLERICAL LIBRARY.

Price 6s. each Volume.

I.

THREE HUNDRED OUTLINES OF SERMONS ON THE NEW TESTAMENT.

"Will come as a godsend to many an overworked preacher."—*Ecclesiastical Gazette.*

II.

OUTLINES OF SERMONS ON THE OLD TESTAMENT.

"Excellently well done. The discourses of the most eminent divines of the day are dissected, and their main thoughts presented in a very compact and suggestive form."—*Methodist Recorder.*

III.

PULPIT PRAYERS BY EMINENT PREACHERS.

"The prayers are, in all cases, exceedingly beautiful, and cannot fail to be read with interest and profit, apart from the special purpose in view."—*Rock.*

IV.

OUTLINE SERMONS TO CHILDREN.

With Numerous Anecdotes.

"Nearly a hundred sermons, by twenty-nine eminent men. They are remarkably well written, and most interesting."—*Rock.*

V.

ANECDOTES ILLUSTRATIVE OF NEW TESTAMENT TEXTS.

"This is one of the most valuable books of anecdote that we have ever seen. There is hardly one anecdote that is not of first-rate quality."—*Christian Leader.*

VI.

EXPOSITORY SERMONS ON THE OLD TESTAMENT.

"Sermons of very unusual merit, requiring from us emphatic praise.—*Literary Churchman.*

THE CLERICAL LIBRARY.

Price 6s. each Volume.

VII.
EXPOSITORY SERMONS ON THE NEW TESTAMENT.

"These sermons, collected together from the best sources, represent the ablest among our public orators."—*Irish Ecclesiastical Gazette.*

VIII.
PLATFORM AIDS.

"Just the book to give to some overworked pastor."—*Christian.*

IX.
NEW OUTLINES OF SERMONS ON THE NEW TESTAMENT.

By *EMINENT PREACHERS.*

Hitherto unpublished.

"They have a freshness and vivacity which are specially taking."—*Sword and Trowel.*

X.
ANECDOTES ILLUSTRATIVE OF OLD TESTAMENT TEXTS.

"An excellent selection, likely to prove most useful to preachers."—*English Churchman.*

XI.
NEW OUTLINES OF SERMONS ON THE OLD TESTAMENT.

"Not only are they excellent specimens of condensed sermons, but hardly without exception they are striking, vigorous, and fresh in treatment and in thought."—*Literary World.*

XII.
OUTLINES OF SERMONS FOR SPECIAL OCCASIONS.

By *EMINENT PREACHERS.*

"Sermons from such miscellaneous sources could hardly fail to be varied and comprehensive as these undoubtedly are, nor could they fail to exhibit eloquence, originality, or spirituality."—*Rock.*

The Theological Educator.

Fcap. 8vo, 2s. 6d. each Volume.

AN INTRODUCTION TO THE OLD TESTAMENT.

By the Rev. *C. H. H. WRIGHT, D.D.*

"The work is of brief compass, and covers a vast field of study, but the necessary compression has been done with the skill of one experienced in the needs of students."—*Scotsman.*

THE WRITERS OF THE NEW TESTAMENT.

Their Style and Characteristics.

By the Rev. *WILLIAM HENRY SIMCOX, M.A.*

"One of the choicest productions of English scholarship in recent years."—*Manchester Examiner.*

THE LANGUAGE OF THE NEW TESTAMENT.

BY THE SAME AUTHOR.

"The most living grammar of the New Testament we have."—*Expositor.*

OUTLINES OF CHRISTIAN DOCTRINE.

By the Rev. *H. C. G. MOULE, M.A.*

AN INTRODUCTION TO THE NEW TESTAMENT.

By the Rev. Professor *MARCUS DODS, D.D.*

"Dr. Marcus Dods has packed away an immense amount of information in a very small space."—*Methodist Recorder.*

An Introduction to THE TEXTUAL CRITICISM OF THE NEW TESTAMENT.

By the Rev. Professor *B. B. WARFIELD, D.D*

"A masterly survey of the whole subject."—*Expositor.*

The Theological Educator.

Price 2s. 6d. each Volume.

A MANUAL OF CHURCH HISTORY.

By the Rev. *A. C. JENNINGS, M.A.*

In Two Volumes.

Vol. I.—From the First to the Tenth Century.
Vol. II.—From the Eleventh to the Nineteenth Century.

"They are small, but they include 'infinite riches in little room.'"—*Globe.*

A MANUAL OF CHRISTIAN EVIDENCES.

By the Rev. Prebendary *C. A. ROW, M.A.*

"A veritable *multum in parvo*, clear, cogent, and concise."—*Saturday Review.*

A MANUAL OF THE BOOK OF COMMON PRAYER.

Showing its History and Contents. For the use of those Studying for Holy Orders and others.

By the Rev. *CHARLES HOLE, B.A.,* King's College, London.

"It is not overloaded with detail, and yet supplies in an admirably compact shape all essential information."—*British Weekly.*

A HEBREW GRAMMAR.

By the Rev. *W. H. LOW, M.A.,* Joint Author of "A Commentary on the Psalms," etc., etc.

"A brief and masterly sketch of Hebrew grammar."—*Literary Churchman.*

AN EXPOSITION OF THE APOSTLES' CREED.

By the Rev. *J. E. YONGE, M.A.,* late Fellow of King's College, Cambridge.

"An able treatise."—*Church Times.*
"A handy book for divinity students, which will give them all the information they want for examination for Orders on the subject which it handles."—*Saturday Review.*

The Household Library of Exposition.

THE GALILEAN GOSPEL.
By Professor *A. B. BRUCE D.D.*
Third Thousand.
Price 3s. 6d.

"We heartily commend this little volume as giving an outline ably drawn of the teaching of Christ."—*Spectator.*

THE SPEECHES OF THE HOLY APOSTLES.
By *DONALD FRASER, D.D.*
Second Thousand.
Price 3s. 6d.

"Exceedingly well done."—*Scottish Review.*

THE LAMB OF GOD.
Expositions in the Writings of St. John.
By *W. ROBERTSON NICOLL, M.A., LL.D.*
Price 2s. 6d.

"A volume of rare beauty and excellence."—*New York Independent.*

THE LORD'S PRAYER.
By *CHARLES STANFORD, D.D.*
Third Thousand.
Price 3s. 6d.

"For spiritual grasp and insight, for wealth of glowing imagery, and for rare felicity of style, it will hold a first place in this valuable series of expository monographs."—*Christian.*

THE LAST SUPPER OF OUR LORD,
And His Words of Consolation to the Disciples.
By *J. MARSHALL LANG, D.D.*, Barony Church, Glasgow.
Third Thousand.
Price 3s. 6d.

"With a rare power of insight—the result, doubtless, of much inward experience—Dr. Lang has entered into the very inmost spirit of the scenes and incidents, the words and feelings, which make up the history of that night."—*Scotsman.*

The Household Library of Exposition.
(CONTINUED.)

THE LAW OF THE TEN WORDS.
By J. OSWALD DYKES, D.D.
Crown 8vo. Price 3s. 6d.

"His style is a singular combination of strength and beauty."—*Literary World.*

THE LIFE OF DAVID.
As Reflected in His Psalms.
By ALEXANDER MACLAREN, D.D., of Manchester.
SEVENTH EDITION.
Price 3s. 6d.

"Just the book we should give to awaken a living and historical interest in the Psalms."—*Guardian.*

THE TEMPTATIONS OF CHRIST.
By G. S. BARRETT, M.A.
Price 3s. 6d.

"Marked alike by careful language and sober thought."—*Guardian.*

THE PARABLES OF OUR LORD.
As Recorded by St. Matthew.
By MARCUS DODS, D.D.
SEVENTH THOUSAND.
Price 3s. 6d.

"There is certainly no better volume on the subject in our language."—*Glasgow Mail.*

THE PARABLES OF OUR LORD.
As Recorded by St. Luke.
By MARCUS DODS, D.D.
SIXTH THOUSAND.
Price 3s. 6d.

"An original exposition, marked by strong common sense and practical exhortation."—*Literary Churchman.*

ISAAC, JACOB, AND JOSEPH.
By MARCUS DODS, D.D.
SIXTH THOUSAND.
Price 3s. 6d.

"The present volume is worthy of the writer's reputation. He deals with the problems of human life and character which these biographies suggest in a candid and manly fashion."—*Spectator.*

WORKS BY DR. R. W. DALE, *of Birmingham.*

FELLOWSHIP WITH CHRIST,

And other Discourses Delivered on Special Occasions.

THIRD THOUSAND.

Crown 8vo, cloth, price 6s.

"These are certainly among the most massive, and, as a consequence, most impressive sermons of the day. Each is a sort of miniature theological treatise, but the theology is alive—as it were, heated through and through by the fires of a mighty conviction, which has become a passion to convince. . . . In these sermons there is a fine universalism; they might be addressed to any audience—academic, professional, commercial, artisan. And to hear them would be to feel that religion is a thing to be believed and obeyed."—*Speaker.*

THE LIVING CHRIST AND THE FOUR GOSPELS.

FIFTH THOUSAND.

Crown 8vo, cloth, price 6s.

"As a man of culture and eloquence he has put the case strongly and well, and it will not be surprising if his book, which is not written, he tells us, for Masters of Arts, but in the first instance for members of his own congregation, and then for all ordinary people who take an interest in such matters, should be the means of convincing many that the assumptions sometimes made about late origin of the Gospels, etc., are utterly unfounded."—*Scotsman.*

LAWS OF CHRIST FOR COMMON LIFE.

FIFTH THOUSAND.

Crown 8vo, price 6s.

"Sound sense and wholesome Christian teaching conveyed in pure, idiomatic, and forcible English."—*Scotsman.*

"A storehouse of wise precepts, a repository of loving counsels—shrewd, practical, and fully cognisant of difficulties and drawbacks; but informed by such sympathy and a sense of Christian brotherhood as should do much to make it acceptable and effective."—*Nonconformist.*

WORKS BY DR. R. W. DALE (continued).

NINE LECTURES ON PREACHING.

Sixth Edition. Crown 8vo, price 6s.

"Admirable lectures, briefly written, earnest and practical."—*Literary Churchman.*

"Dr. Dale's lectures are full of practical wisdom and intense devotion."—*The Expositor.*

THE JEWISH TEMPLE AND THE CHRISTIAN CHURCH.

A Series of Discourses on the Epistle to the Hebrews.

Eighth Edition. Crown 8vo, price 6s.

"Wholesomer sermons than these it is almost impossible to conceive. Mr. Dale's preaching has always been remarkable for moral energy and fervour, but here this characteristic rises to its highest power."—*Expositor.*

THE EPISTLE TO THE EPHESIANS.

Its Doctrines and Ethics.

Sixth Edition. Crown 8vo, price 7s. 6d.

"The terse and vigorous style, rising on occasion into a manly and impressive eloquence, of which Mr. Dale is known to be a master, gives lucid expression to thought that is precise, courageous, and original."—*Spectator.*

WEEK-DAY SERMONS.

Fifth Edition. Crown 8vo, price 3s. 6d.

"Dr. Dale is certainly an admirable teacher of Christian ethics. He is, perhaps, the greatest living successor of the Apostle James. In this volume he appears at his best."—*Christian.*

THE TEN COMMANDMENTS.

Sixth Edition. Crown 8vo, price 5s.

"Full of thought and vigour."—*Spectator.*

IMPRESSIONS OF AUSTRALIA.

Crown 8vo, cloth, price 5s.

"Dr. Dale's articles ... constitute one of the most sensible books about Australia.... The book is readable, and indeed excellent."—*Athenæum.*

THE NEW EVANGELICALISM AND THE OLD.

Cloth, price 1s.

"It has more in it than many an elaborate treatise; it suggests by every sentence; it is throughout succinct, pregnant, masterly."—*British Weekly.*

WORKS BY REV. PROF. MARCUS DODS, D.D.

ERASMUS, AND OTHER ESSAYS.

Crown 8vo, cloth, price 5s.

"Professor Marcus Dods is a theologian, and much more. The essays in this volume show him, not for the first time, as a man of much reading, of broad and genial sympathies, refined but liberal judgment, possessed of no little literary culture, and keenly appreciative of literary and mental power in other men even when they do not happen to belong to his own school."—*Scotsman.*

MOHAMMED, BUDDHA, AND CHRIST.

SIXTH THOUSAND.

Crown 8vo, cloth, price 3s. 6d.

THE PRAYER THAT TEACHES TO PRAY.

SEVENTH EDITION.

Crown 8vo, price 2s. 6d.

"It is highly instructive, singularly lucid, and unmistakably for quiet personal use."—*Clergyman's Magazine.*

ISRAEL'S IRON AGE.

Sketches from the Period of the Judges.

SIXTH EDITION.

Crown 8vo, price 3s. 6d.

"Powerful lectures. This is a noble volume, full of strength."—*Nonconformist.*

WORKS BY DR. W. M. TAYLOR, of New York.

THE PARABLES OF OUR SAVIOUR.

Expounded and Illustrated.

THIRD EDITION.

Crown 8vo, cloth, price 7s. 6d.

"We have many books on the Parables of our Lord, but few which so thoroughly as this condense within their covers the best teaching contained in the various commentaries written to elucidate their meaning."—*English Churchman.*

THE MIRACLES OF OUR SAVIOUR.

Expounded and Illustrated.

By the Same Author.

Crown 8vo, cloth, price 7s. 6d.

"Dr. Taylor takes up each miracle separately, sets forth in a vivid and graphic manner the circumstances attending it, and then proceeds to draw out in impressive language the lessons it suggests."—*Scotsman.*

LONDON: HODDER & STOUGHTON, 27, PATERNOSTER ROW, E.C